I0462762

nuclear brands

15 years
of history
reflections
+ prediction

SMoss

'HcT! Press

Nuclear Brands

15 years of history, reflection + predictions

ISBN 9781075892769

An 'HcT! book

Portrait of SMoss by Paula Sweet

diganzi.com

DiGanZi

'HcT! Press

"...nuclear brands are clearly understood at their inception; successfully express simple and identifiable core precepts; contain explosive and transformative ideas; or cause sudden and powerful conceptual detonations in the popular awareness."

I've been searching for nuclear brands since the turn of the century, but I didn't know it at first. I couldn't even say what they were. Initially I was tracking the expanding conversation about branding, trying to figure out what the whole thing meant.

With the luxury of retrospect, I realize that *nuclear brands* are clearly understood at their inception; successfully express simple and identifiable core precepts; contain explosive and transformative ideas; or cause sudden and powerful conceptual detonations in the popular awareness. They occur intentionally or unwittingly, by design or happenstance.

Back in 2004 I sent out a 2-page crib sheet to a select bundle of clients who had been asking questions, a time when the brand dialogue was just heating up. I found myself simply wrestling to keep up with terminology, and tried to make sense of the connections. I collected quotes and vocabulary over the course of the 12-month interval, then sat down at the keyboard every January and madly set to writing. I was locked in - people were waiting and I couldn't interrupt the flow. In 2018 I reduced the interval to 6-months between letters.

At the outset, globalisation, sustainability, valuation, measurement, CSR, and brand architecture occupied the largest part of my reporting. I heard little about the ethical dialogue or the McElroy Memo, which dictated the thinking in the business schools. It positioned all brand behavior under the umbrella of fast-moving consumer goods (FMCGs). From my perspective the theory of brands, the ideological underpinnings and philosophical process, were more important than the bottom-line drivers which appeared to obsess educators. You'd be amazed at what comes forward after you write an annual letter on branding for 15 years straight. It's possible to track world history and current events by looking across these letters. You witness ideas as they dawn, terms as they migrate into the popular vocabulary, and dramatic shifts in consumer attitude. You hear all the new slang. Celebrities appear and disappear, companies rise and fall. Brands which stretch the imagination establish themselves. The big dogs demonstrate arrogance, and then receive a fusillade of flack. You're immersed in jargon, some seasonal, some enduring. Place branding never leaves the conversation. Big promises are made. Human folly confounds strategists and marketers. And such a fuss emerges over influencers.

By the advent of internet-based communication, branding became a larger part of public discourse. Terms like 'authenticity' and 'purpose' and 'experience' were liberally bandied about. The Medinge Group, a think-tank I headed from 2004-2012, originated an awards program called "Brands With A Conscience." Everyone knew they needed a brand, everyone wanted one, but most people couldn't say what one was. This motivated me to publish the answers to my yearly penultimate question "What Is A Brand?" in a single collection. I took a lot of flack for it. People wanted a long book filled with superfluous exposition, like an airport bookstore business shelf title or a textbook. But the collection demonstrated that the answer wasn't a consistent or stable one; the answer depended on who you were asking, and when you asked. Brands, it turned out, were ever-evolving and elastic entities, subject to the agenda of the interrogated. The book is now in its 4th edition.

Following a trip to India in 2008 I ventured an idea that brands had become too loud. You can see the first remarks on Quiet Brands in a short item which appears on page 196. My opinion remains unchanged eleven years later. The louder brands are, the less I trust them. Brand credibility built on advertising, marketing and slick veneer indicates either something worth hiding, or nothing behind the facade.

At a later point in time literate society ceased to value face-to-face interactions, subordinated human contact to 160-character messages and chose to believe every digitally propagated assertion. I refer of course to the popularization of the phenomenon called social media. A bizarre democratization took hold, the equivalent of an atomic explosion of ephemera, meaninglessness and obsolescence. Does anyone remember MySpace, LonelyGirl15 or Farmville?

What endured were red flags raised about privacy, or the glut of propaganda which had become a regular part of digital life. Further anxieties multiplied over the ill effects of automation, AI, AR and VR. With the reductive devolution of eloquence and an over-reliance on technology, transgressive symbols like emoticons altered the ability to shape complex thoughts. Such radical transformation of language feeds directly into how identity is communicated. Can I not do better than a smiley face? Nuclear brands carry the messages.

My hope is that digital junkies ultimately understand the false promise of influencers and the spiritual bankruptcy embedded in the brands they represent. Thinking people will need to abandon abrogation of responsibility to AI and the Internet Of Things. The value of personal data being harvested by apparently innocent and well-meaning brands is still greatly underestimated. Wars used to be fought by murdering huge populations and obliterating massive amounts of real property, but no longer. With such a devaluation of physical assets the new weapons of mass destruction are data-plunder and rampant digital and device dependency. Cyber warfare and the nuclear brands that nourish it have the power to re-fashion the world. May we come to our senses in time.

But allow me to reserve comment until 2034, after the next fifteen years of brand letters have been written. By then there ought to be more to say.

SMoss
Vicenza, Italy
July 2019

2019.1

"Let no new thing arise." - Spanish toast

"I wish I'd invented a lawn mower." - Mikhail Kalashnikov

"Hungry man is an angry man." - James Joyce, *Ulysses*

Spent too much time on Oumuamua, where I met an omnichannel ethnonationalist prankster who tried to get me to take a significant position in malfeasium. She produced geospatial evidence, exercised plausible deniability, accused me of *pseudologia fantastica*. I said: it must be attributable to quantitative tightening, the consequence of incessant surveillance and interaction.

Updates on last season's hot topics

"*Odi et amo. Excrucior!*" (I hate you and I love you. I am tortured!) - Catullus 85

Advertising

If you can trust developers, there is a direct correlation between the reduction of stress and the amount that passengers spend at **airports**. That's why you may soon discover yourself unconsciously engaging in compulsive retail therapy while waiting for flights. Get ready to encounter improved shopping and dining options and food courts more reminiscent of Whole Foods than Burger King. The big focus will be in emerging markets - shoppers spend 30% more at some airports, which helps to keep aeronautical charges down. The state of US airports infrastructure is dismal. The biggest challenge remains the moderating of information overload while motivating purchase. One thing that won't change: yowling video screens.

Payless pushed *the social-experiment genre* to new heights, persuading a group of influencers to pay up to $600 for shoes worth $20 at a bogus pop-up luxury store fake-branded Palessi. The agency explained that they wanted to make a cultural statement and remind consumers the brand was still a place to shop for affordable fashion. All the money was returned, and the influencers allowed to keep the shoes. The agency then created a series of ads broadcast on cable and social media showing the prank victims' reactions. Following the campaign, Payless filed for Chapter 11 and began to shut down 2,500 real stores.

Seasonal **luxury campaigns** ran the gambit from enhanced technology concepts to embracing diversity. Tiffany focused on nostalgia; Gucci employed animated digital paintings with AR and VR installations; Burberry showcased its new orange and white logo print in a digital campaign with a counterfeit mistake. But Balmain attracted the most attention with its trio of influencers, each with her own IG account and army of followers. Media took note. After which the company was forced to reveal that the three were actually custom-designed virtual digital models.

Should you detect an unusual 7 degree backslant, gaps in each letterform and element of *desirable difficulty* while browsing stray advertising copy, you may have uncovered evidence that the brand boys are at work again on your consciousness. An Australian university's behavioral business lab and design school created **Sans Forgetica**, a typeface purported to use psychological and design theories to aid memory retention. It cannot be called beautiful. Compared to classic Bodoni it looks like an unresolved, airheaded stencil font.

Tobacco products shall not be advertised in the UK, where Ecig use is championed by British public health agencies. In the USA brand recognition is driven by advertising, the market dominated by a fashionably-designed USB-shaped device called **Juul**, used by 70% of US vapers. The Brits watch closely as the brand debuts on their shores, even with such products regulated at a lower nicotine content. Teenagers the earliest adopters, represent the highest growth rate of users.

The **lifestyle brand** bandwagon lumbers on. You may recall our friends at Chipotle suffered an enduring hit to public confidence in 2015. Last year they announced Chipotle was no longer just a food brand but a *purpose-driven* lifestyle brand. Everybody loves that language. Godiva will leverage their culinary expertise to expand beyond chocolates. Blue Apron, IHOP and Pizza Hut now describe themselves as lifestyle brands, in hopes that they represent something larger than the goods they sell. Since millennials already surpass boomers in trips taken, a choice strategy involves lifestyle co-branding with hospitality to support this message. Hottest partnerships across categories: Armani, Baccarat, Bulgari, Equinox, Muji, Nobu, Paramount Pictures, Restoration Hardware and Versace, all to offer themed hotels, most with shopping options. While promotion centers on conventional media platforms, these brands will focus more on event-driven strategies. Endurance and consistency required. A woman approached Samuel Johnson - who never bathed - at a party and said, "Dr. Johnson, you smell." "Incorrect, madam," Johnson replied. "I stink. You smell." One Johnsonian lifestyle property plans a dedicated room screening comedies all day, each floor with its own unique fragrance, scented elevators and LPs played in the lobby - when the album changes, a new fragrance gets spritzed.

"Hypotheses non fingo." (I feign no hypotheses.) - Isaac Newton

AI

While **Natural Language Understanding** struggles to puzzle out exactly what humans mean when they speak, it's too early to crack the complexity and ambiguity of verbal communication. The process necessarily begins with a devaluation of language. At the moment NLU focuses on 100 labeled examples, of approximate emoticon grade. From this starting point - since computers with their great dimensionality can handle information far faster and in much greater volume - neural networks form a pattern of recognition, simultaneously missing other worthy examples of what might be called *coded language*. The more the machines can understand, the more the demand for human input will fall. New metaphors will naturally form. One early casualty are call center workers, whose jobs have already been taken by chatbots. M&S in the UK receives around a million phone inquiries a month; they moved 100 switchboard staff to other duties and replaced them with synths. The next evolutionary leap will come with *emotion analysis systems*, which can figure out the moment when you reach the breaking point in the phone tree and you want to kill someone, anyone. Chalk it up to the commodification of emotion, subjective territory where machine learning doesn't fear to tread. Argumentation is a uniquely human attribute. IBM Project Debater squared off against a carbon-based entity, told pre-programmed jokes, had the temerity to suggest its opponent was lying, and used classic rhetorical technique to disprove a rival argument before it was made. IBM insisted the software could be applied as a weapon against fake news, but the computer lost the debate.

An **AI-generated digital print portrait** on canvas developed by the French art collective Obvious (Not to be confused with *Obviously*, an influencer agency) was offered by Christie's at auction, estimated to sell at $7k-10k. Created using a model called Generative Adversarial Network, the work was based on 15,000 scanned likenesses done between the 14th and 20th centuries, and intended to democratize the model and legitimize AI-produced art. The collective generated works until it was able to fool a test designed *to distinguish whether an image was human or machine made*, another example of the false objectivity biased by the prejudices of the creators. The first-to-market advantage prevailed: the piece sold at $432,500.

"Tell me, George, if you had it to do all over, would you fall in love with yourself again?" - Oscar Levant to Gershwin

Celebrity

Apparently ghouls love clickbait stories. High Google traffic numbers and a pattern of base searches lead one to suspect that Alphabet is actually a zombie company, since it was so fixated on the **suicides** of Anthony Bourdain and Kate Spade. It is a truth universally acknowledged that the undead hunger for headlines designed to feed search engine demand. This validates rumors of an unseemly and vaguely cannibalistic desire to read about the intimate last moments of a life. Search optimized headlines, once more moderate in tone, now reach for traffic at the expense of editorial morality. Zombies never give up potential revenue in exchange for professional ethics. They have a narcotic, amoral dependency which nudges users toward bloodthirsty extremism.

"Oh, the room didn't used to be as nice as this until I removed that hill over there. I just hated the way it reflected light."- Bunny Mellon

Epiphanies

Is it true that **Amazon** has an inherent advantage that undermines fair competition? Bezos Inc. now employs more than half a million people worldwide and powers much of the internet through its cloud computing division. It dominates the product and food supply chains and has more revenue than FB, Google and Twitter combined. People like its speedy delivery and low prices. None dare whisper the word monopoly. In a new partnership with Marriott, Alexa voice-powered devices will soon share your junior suite, deputized to order room service, book spa treatments, play music, adjust lighting and temperature and listen in on your intimate conversations. Amazon already controls ⅔ of the consumer smart speaker market. Next up: wanton data collection in cars and offices. Amazon was urged to halt sales of its facial recognition software, but not before the product sold to a number of police forces. There's a new program which aims at helping people start their own businesses delivering Amazon packages. You get access to branded data products, vehicles and uniforms. The kicker: *exclusivity*, meaning you're not an employee, but you can't work for anyone else.

Chinese artist **Cao Fei** created a video work at MoMA PS1 about a quasi-fictional high-tech warehouse near Shanghai staffed by only 2 workers. Addressing the trend toward fewer and fewer people doing the work of manufacturing or distribution, the artist confronted issues of massive dislocation, technological control, mass surveillance, a future where everything is constantly scanned and scored, the coming challenges of isolation, loneliness and joblessness. Ironically, the final steps of this conceptual logistic chain are still more reliant on humans.

For decades **Coca-Cola** flourished without direct contact with customers. Now the paradigm changes with its $3.9bn purchase of Costa from Whitbread. Coke is disposing of its bottling operations to independents. Coffee houses ground communities and provide places where people can meet. As the pleasures of the city have been largely reduced to consumerism, the beverage giant is taking a clue from Apple's retail stores, the most influential channels for brand building and humanising its image. Costa also has over 8000 vending machines selling branded coffee, a channel Coke already understands well.

**"If everything is under control you are just not driving fast enough."
- Sir Stirling Moss**

In its strategy to court millennials **Dolce & Gabbana** typically uses IG stars for its runway shows, especially in China. A series of unusually swift IG reposts, with charges of racism flooded China before an upcoming show. There had been fallout over an earlier controversial ad campaign, where Chinese models struggled with cannoli and chopsticks, and the brand endured accusations of offensive language. Yet IG is banned in China, as well as is FB, YouTube, Google and Twitter. Stefano Gabbana insisted his account had been hacked, then cancelled the fashion show. D&G is so frequently the subject of boycotts in China that its website sells $295 t-shirts with a red heart inviting people to #boycottdolcegabanna. Online outrage is suspected to be stoked by state-controlled media.

An olfactory brand extension took a seasonal front seat when **KFC** released a limited-edition Yule log fragranced like the chain's famous fried chicken. Flavored with 11 proprietary herbs and spices, it perfumed your holiday home for an appetizing $18.99.

Management consultants continue to transform their reputations. Over the objections of three influential partners, **McKinsey** violated South African contracting law with Midas-sized payments channeled to the Indian Gupta family. The lavishness of the payouts and lack of public accountability altered perception of the firm as a hidden power with a prestigious face. This was the biggest government procurement in South African history, 1064 locomotives. The government hired McKinsey not knowing what the final bill would be. On another front, **Accenture** agreed to buy Droga5, the independent ad agency based in New York, responsible for the much-derided ad campaign that not-so-subtly equated Coke Zero with *erythroxylon coca*. Marketing is no longer simply about coming up with attention-grabbing ads. Suddenly the aim is to create an Uber-like, Amazon-like experience in retail stores or online.

In its first 3 days of release, **Red Dead Redemption 2** earned $725m, the highest grossing opening weekend of any entertainment product ever. To place that in some kind of context, the *Aquaman* movie had a worldwide gross of $332m in its first week of release. Despite its reputation as a psychologically destructive hobby, gaming's no longer a second-class cultural medium. Gamers typically devote 60 hours or more to these products. Rockstar, the game's creator, would like you to believe they are *existential journeys* built on the rhythms of survival, and not a way to avoid responsibility.

What's left to nosh? Not to spoil your appetite, but the culprit turned out to be anything containing whey powder provided by Associated Milk Producers Inc., a Minnesota company. After a salmonella risk was identified, Mendelez, the snack food producer recalled **Ritz Crackers, Ritz Bits Cheese, Ritz cheese cracker sandwiches and Ritz bacon cracker sandwiches**. Other brands implicated: Flowers Foods, Hungry Man, Kellogg's Honey Smacks cereal (100 people sickened), Pepperidge Farms. And *monsieur* is advised not to order the Caesar Salad in selected territories: E. coli was found lurking in Romaine lettuce.

Facing accusations of commodification of local neighborhood culture **Target** in NYC's East Village exhibited signs of bald-faced brand hijacking. A brand activation recreated the iconic CBGB facade and fake storefronts intended to look like the mom-and-pops that were once a staple of the neighborhoods, on the street level of snazzy new condos. Target even distributed replicas of co-opted vintage newspaper designs. Upstairs the smallest new studio rents for $3681/month. There's a flourishing Newark Airport franchise: CBGB Lounge and Bar, dishing up all-American fare, who also licensed the iconic signature from the estate of Hilly Kristal, the punk bar's legendary owner.

The great hope of co-living, co-working spaces and millennial residences blurs the lines between home, work and play. The myth of futureproofing hasn't yet been validated. IKEA has Space10, a lab for testing prototypes and explores ideas for more sustainable ways of existing. One hopeful rethink sought a better life using *smaller* shared houses. For $3k/month rent, a millennial could get a private studio including utilities, cleaning, laundry, shared kitchens, offices, and recreational spaces. But millennials want to own, not rent - something the sharing economy doesn't permit at the entry level. As millennials' digital connections grow, they increasingly crave human interaction, hence they're always seeking community. Co-living models are still restricted to the relatively wealthy. Imposing rules on the over-entitled is difficult. Participation is encouraged, but not enforced. Don't anybody tell **WeWork**, who just bought an office cleaning business and whose losses now are almost $2bn a year.

"Of all ghosts the ghost of our old loves are the worst." - Arthur Conan Doyle

IP

In a dustup between outlaw bikers and IP lawyers, who do you bet will win? Trademarks, unlike copyrights and patents, have no enduring value apart from their use, a fact well-known to the **Mongols**, a bikerider club also characterized as one of the most dangerous criminal enterprises in the country. In a racketeering trial in Orange County CA, prosecutors sued to allow seizure of the group's unifying symbol, which has been occasionally licensed or hijacked. The Mongols' mark is registered with the US Patent and Trademark Office. Asset forfeiture allows the law to seize goods used in the commission of crimes. Other victims of this variety of identity theft are Hell's Angels, who have successfully defended rights to their image in infringement cases against Alexander McQueen, Amazon, Saks, ToysRUs and the Walt Disney Company. Biker dudes rule™.

"Simpler to leave stuff for when I am dead." - Ernest Hemingway

Later, 'gator.

Alan Abel, 94, tricks no more. The original proto prankster, with the help of a dozen accomplices successfully faked his own death in 1980, causing the NYTimes to publish, then retract his obit. A master psychologist, keen strategist and possessor of a bevy of aliases, the former jazz drummer, stand-up comic, writer, campus lecturer, and filmmaker left behind an opus of performance art, self-promotion, social commentary, dalliances with the press and simple mischief. His greatest triumph: the nonexistent Society for Indecency to Naked Animals. But he may have overstayed his welcome and there was no profit in duplicity. Abel made barely a living hoaxing, and perhaps yelled "Fire!" in one too many auditoriums.

And now ladies and gentlemen, **Rosa Bouglione**, 107, catches the spotlight for the last time. According to her own publicity, the undisputed queen of the circus world was born in a horse-drawn caravan in Belgium. She always understood the notion that the show must go on. She chose to be married in a lion's cage, then spent her honeymoon performing with Buffalo Bill Cody's Wild West Show. She worked behind the scenes later in career, and moved to a house around the corner from the family business in 1984. Well into her old age she faithfully attended matinees and her funeral was held in the center ring of the Cirque d'Hiver.

Kitty O'Neill, 72, made the ultimate leap. A legendary stunt performer, she retired in 1982 at the age of 36 years old. A 5-

foot-3, 100 lb. dynamo, O'Neill lost her hearing at 4 months old from measles and mumps. But her mother taught her lip reading rather than sign language and urged her to run and swim, dive and leap from high places. She broke world speed records in rocket cars, dragsters, motorcycles, dune buggies and on waterskis. In her life she drifted from place to place and lover to lover, endured an abusive husband who ripped her off, even lost two fingers in a motorcycle accident. When she moved over to the stunt world she jumped off a 10-story building for *Wonder Woman*. Mattel even fashioned an action-figure doll of her. She was set on fire, and then rolled a car three times and landed it right side up for the film *Smokey and the Bandit*. After that stunt she was heard to utter her most famous catch-phrase, "Easy. Great. Do again."

"But decay is written into the genes of cities." - Lawrence Osborne

Place branding

The city of **Acquetico, Italy** had no intention to generate cash, and simply wanted to protect people's safety on their main road. After residents complained, the town of 120 set up a trial speed camera and recorded 58,568 speeding offenses in the first two weeks. Nearly half of all cars traveling the route were speeding in the 50km/h zone - some drivers clocked at 135km/h.

Dogs trained to guard rhinoceroses in the **Eastern Cape Province, South Africa** heard a pride of lions active nearby in an area densely packed with thorn bushes. Later, Rangers came upon the remains of as many as three men, suspected members of traveling poaching gangs for whom rhino horn has huge value. Once lions have taken down a human, you cannot be on the ground with them. The lion population is stable and doesn't understand *karma*, while the poacher population is growing, and are better equipped with earthly tools than ever.

Once upon a time there was a country Trump didn't want to invade. It was a regional hub where organized crime never touched the daily lives of every citizen. State officials kept a careful watch on criminal activity, and no illegal drugs poured across its borders. Even drug production was at an all-time low. It wasn't a haven for ex-guerrillas from the Middle East, and nobody smuggled the cheapest gasoline in the world across its borders, on which they didn't make a higher markup than on a kilo of Bolivian Marching Powder. Free press and television were in place, inflation was at a manageable rate, and transparency and accountability was normal. State coffers were full, leaving little incentive to steal. There was an efficient and functioning power grid and the stores were filled with food. Medicine was freely available to all. Responsible policy protected the Amazon, and limits to illegal mining for gold, coltan and other natural resources were enforced. There had been no significant brain drain, and no refugees could be found in Colombia, Brazil and Guyana. So, what's your brilliant idea for nation-branding **Venezuela** this year?

Passengers on bus in **Paris, France** wouldn't move to allow a wheelchair-bound man with MS to get in. The driver asked all the passengers to leave the bus. Once it was empty he invited Francois Le Berre, the man in the *fauteuil roulant*, to board, then drove off. The passengers at the curb were left to wait for the next bus.

London has its Gherkin, and LA has the Blue Whale. Construction on a famed tower in Italy began in 1173, but almost immediately its foundation began to shift. The tower was completed, compensating for the change in baseline, but its shape became one which recollects a curvaceous tropical fruit. It took eight hundred years for the tilt to reach 4.5 meters from the true vertical and in 1990 the tower was closed. Over the intervening years a number of tubes were installed underground on the side the tower leans away from, a process involving the removal of soil by drilling very carefully. A half a degree of lean has been recovered. Now that the tower has regained some verticality, isn't it only appropriate that the landmark adopt the name The Leaning Banana of **Pisa**.

If you are planning on retirement in **Maricopa County CA, USA**, you may want to rethink the quality issues of elder care. A 92-year old woman shot and killed her son in order to avoid being sent into an assisted living facility there. The son, 72, had wanted her to change residences because she had become difficult to live with. She concealed two firearms in her bathrobe before confronting and blasting him, then wrestled with his girlfriend, who got away and called the cops. Police found her in a reclining chair in her bedroom, where she stated she deserved whatever happened to her next, undoubtedly a free assisted living facility behind bars.

"I do not discuss the nature of my business or personal relationships." - Gabriel Schulze

Privacy

Robin Hood hid in Sherwood Forest, and **hackers** use aliases. The latter suddenly experience remorse and regret when their real identity is drawn into the open and they come to the realization that it's a job with no future. Oversharing online is the new hazard, and everybody is vulnerable, so much that it takes more energy to remain anonymous than to stay hidden. FB expanded its existing bug bounty with a program that specifically targets data abuse, and offered high legal incentives for joining the real world. That's what happens when you eliminate the Sheriff of Nottingham and morph into cybersecurity experts.

While the US excels at data collection and the science of reselling it for profit, **China** refines the tools. The fear of being watched is the most powerful tool of all. By 2020 a national video surveillance network in the Middle Kingdom will be *omnipresent, fully networked, always working and fully controllable*. A complex prototype system already tracks pupils in one state school. Besides the usual quantification, the system monitors facial expressions to see how children engage in class to predict which pupils are likely to underperform. Out in the real world, facial recognition, and the monitoring of mobile payments is constant. At a pop concert in eastern China, facial recognition technology picked out four men accused of crimes. Keyser Söze would need to adopt yet another walk to fool new gait recognition algorithms.China also runs a Social Credit system scoring citizens on past behavior. Good scores confer benefits, while a poor social credit score could jeopardize university placement, rule out certain jobs, exile one to a debtor's list, limit travel. The system already bars 11m people from buying airline or high speed rail tickets. One region requires mandatory mobile-surveillance software installed on residents' phones. Public spending at this scale is proving a windfall for Chinese security companies. There's a whole market to be plumbed in augmented reality glasses, aimed at consumers rather than law enforcement.

In the most significant supply chain attack known, sinister forces in Chinese factories - who are estimated to make 75% of world's mobile phones - secretly nested **tiny microchips** on motherboards bound for America, compromising major banks, government contractors and the US Department of Defense. The Minister of Foreign Affairs reiterated that China is a resolute defender of cybersecurity.

Clorox paid to license thermometers that synch up with smartphone apps, which then indicate ZIP codes around the country where increases in fever are detected. The company then directs more ads to those areas. Televisions track what we are watching and allow advertisers to target *other devices*. Products are recommended based on keywords harvested from conversations. **Amazon** has submitted a patent application outlining how a company could recommend chicken soup or cough drops if an Echo device detects symptoms like coughing or sniveling. If the device senses boredom, it might suggest a visit to the movies. A digital adman protested that this is not advertising in the strict sense of advertising.

"No picture and it didn't happen." - Millennial truism

Social Media

Natasha Aponte surreptitiously used **Tinder** to match up online with 150-200 guys. She didn't mention she intended to stage a pop-up competition, invited them all to meet her for a first date in Union Square NYC. The desperate and gullible showed up with flowers and letters, excited to hook up with her. She first disqualified men shorter than 5-foot 10, those named Jimmy, or who had been dumped in their previous relationship, then made the remainder do one-armed pushups for her. She later claimed the stunt was engineered for a purpose *other than getting a date*: making a video of the event. The dudes were not happy. One candidate who refused to compete said it was funny and obviously successful.

Marketers love **nanoinfluencers**, folks who have as few as 1000 followers, but are willing to advertise products. They're easy to deal with, say whatever the company tells them to and are substantially cheaper than the original variety. Obviously - no relation to the art collective *Obvious* - a full-service influencer marketing agency, tracks and measures what works and doesn't. Influencers with more than a million social followers command $60k for providing apparel companies with one IG post and three IG stories and for being photographed during fashion weeks. The little players can charge $500 for two IG posts for a product like men's shaving cream, and must agree to keep it on their feed for a certain number of weeks and use certain keywords provided by marketing. On IG alone, the market for *celebrity endorsement* is said to be worth $1.07bn. The top tier of influence is saturated, and losing the homespun quality. The guys at the bottom of the food chain look like the land of opportunity. Brands also double down on **twin influencers**. They're an easy hook, a basic marketing tool which can be sold as twice the visual impressions. A pair of influential replicant Canadian sisters insist a picture of two girls is going to stand out when they look more similar. Approached by a manager and a company ready to sponsor them, they discovered that thousands could be charged for an endorsement post. Matching bikinis and the same poses get the biggest response.

Big tobacco blows sophisticated smoke on advertising rules governing online platforms. A research team at USC analyzed social media in 10 countries by looking for *hashtags that connect to tobacco* brands. 123 hashtags were viewed 25bn times around the world. The FTC petitioned against four companies for deceptive social media marketing. All the companies claimed they did not market to minors, where they were prohibited from employing branded content. Social is thick with misleading practices. Followers are led to believe that social media endorsements are independent. Similar behavior has been reported on dating websites, online hotel booking, car rental intermediaries, secondary ticketing agencies.

Financial mismanagement of donations and fraud are problems for **online crowdfunding sites**. A homeless man in Philly gave a couple his last $20 for gas. They started an on-line fundraiser to help him and in nine months they raised over $400,000. The couple held on to the money, some of which the homeless man's lawyer claims they spent on vacations and a new BMW.

What limits to online propriety? Now **Facebook**'s a bane on society. Their big *superposter* spews hate like a 'coaster, and does it with vicious variety. Forget all the do-gooder memes, this brand's about wickeder dreams. They're weak on the facts and high on attacks, encouraging rightwing extremes. The towns where the algo is used eventually find themselves bruised. Once high on engagement, it ends with derangement, then innocent people abused. Anxiety now runs amuck, all this in pursuit of a buck. No moderate voices are heard for good choices. It's lining the pockets of Zuck. And sowing the seeds of confusion. Our data we share in delusion. Split up into groups they put us through hoops. Social media's one big illusion.

FB is accustomed to playing both ends against the middle. Black Elevation was an orchestrated political influence campaign, aimed at sowing divisions among Americans ahead of the midterm elections. Can't say definitely who did it, but it mirrored previous efforts by the Internet Research Agency, a Russian organization that tried to manipulate voters in the United States ahead of the 2016 elections. The posts tapped into negative, primal emotions like anger or fear, which perform best, and showed an increased sophistication in understanding American culture and the use of technology and colloquialisms of the activist community. The fake group aimed at left-wing activists in the USA, scheduled rallies, got attendance and coverage and went so far as to advertise for an Event Coordinator.

"I like smooth shiny girls, hardboiled and loaded with sin." - Raymond Chandler

Trends

You know that *text and voice messaging are dead* when IG squares off against YouTube with a new standalone **video** app. IGTV intends to generate revenue through advertising, which will then be split with the creators. FB announced the launch of an internal agency to connect influencers with brands who wish to sponsor their work.

In **Shanghai**, street wear has assumed the dimensions of obsession. The city's turned into a public stage for the latest fashion concepts in China. Yo'Hood, a multi-faceted branded media empire that started as a magazine, encompasses street culture, e-commerce, festivals, editorial, offline and retail. They even run a yearly event, kind of like Burning Man for Chinese millennials. Major criteria for their attention: regular posting, especially retail spaces *worth photographing*, stores designed to impress and appear on social media. The brand loves unexpected collaborations, like a delivery app which combines street wear with takeaway food. Cultural value is as important as commercial value.

"What, you gave it to that *existentialist*?" - Edith Piaf to Charles Aznavour, enraged to find he'd given a song to Juliette Gréco

Vocabulary and concepts entering the mainstream in 2019

Algorithmic governance - suspicious idea for a new way to manage the economy and society (*See also* **algorithmic transparency**)

Amenitize - real estate developer's technique to like add shit Millennials want in offices and residences

Co-ordinated inauthentic behaviour - official reason given for removal of 32 pages and accounts from FB and IG

Deepfake - a portmanteau of "deep learning" and "fake", an artificial intelligence-based human image synthesis technique. It creates fake celebrity or revenge porn by combining and superimposing source images and videos.

Foss - Zuckerberg's inner circle, allies known colloquially at FB as "Friends of Sheryl Sandberg"

Fundamental attribution error - a cognitive bias that leads us to attribute behavior we don't like to other people's characters, rather than circumstances or outside factors.

HENRYs - High Earners Not Rich Yet, new consumer category. *See* HNWIs

Irony poisoning - that which results when heavy social media users lose sight of the line separating trolling from sincere hate

Latency - the time it takes for devices to communicate with one another

Panopticon - the idea that people will follow the rules precisely because they don't know whether they are being watched.

Procatalepsis - a rhetorical technique that involves identifying and disproving a rival argument before it has even been made.

Redpilling - The red and blue pills are cultural memes representing the choice between knowledge, freedom, uncertainty and reality (red) and its opposite, security, happiness, beauty, and blissful illusion (blue). See *The Matrix* (1999)

Smashing - a casual erotic encounter. *"Are we dating, or are we just smashing?"*

Smoking simulating products - industry euphemism for vape pens

Ultracrepidarian sciolist - accusation leveled between warring FT commenters; (*one who criticizes, judges, or gives advice outside the area of his or her expertise*) + (*one who pretends to be knowledgeable and well-informed*)

"I've been married to a communist and a fascist, and neither would take out the garbage." - Zsa Zsa Gabor

What is A Brand?

I've been thinking about quieting brands. The whole discipline has got too numerous, too crowded, too loud. Discretion has exited the dialogue. Beauty doesn't figure. Branding has come down to the commodification and commercialization of a *persona*, just to complete a transaction. It plays to our basest instincts.

A brand is a surrogate for sex.

A brand is a gross means to promote the production of pheromones, endorphins and serotonin.

We can talk about all this later.

2018.2

"Be silent, unless what you have to say is better than silence." - Stoic philosopher's admonition

"Luxury is a form of waste designed to confer status on an essentially useless class of people." - Thorsten Veblen, 1899

"His neck was thin and would wring easily if someone were of a mind." - Robert B. Parker

No collusion? Pardon me, my microparticle might be turning into microfiber, meaning it may have de-yanged my microfinance. Get back to me in a Fortnite, but only if you have wedge issues with digital abrogation.

Update on last year's hot topics

According to its mission statement, it was set up in 2017 for the "creation and commercial exploitation of museums."
- Catherine Hutin-Blay, daughter of the artist's second wife, on the Fondation Picasso

"Post-kiss, it was never going to work. Maybe it was the Doritos." - Monika Gupta

Advertising and PR

A 22-year old self-proclaimed **social media influencer** dissolved into tears after she asked a Dublin hotel for 5-night free stay and was refused. The hotelier responded by an indignant public post. Users, quick to identify her, loosed a barrage of negation characterizing her as a disgusting freeloader. "I was exposed (SO embarrassing)" - while the property faced its own backlash and subsequently banned all bloggers, YouTubers and Instagram stars from its premises. The hotel's proprietor observed that the sense of entitlement is simply too strong in the blogging community. Does this mean influencer marketing is on its last legs or did the hotel simply consult the writer's reviews, where the word *stunning* appears all too frequently?

An online **content clearing house** offers up a book which claims to show how storytelling can help you forge stronger relationships with customers, colleagues *and anyone else in the world you want to reach.* In 208 pages of large text you get useful instructions on how to transform your business, how to talk to other humans, how to stop declaiming into the emptiness and *how to make people love you.* Priced at only $16.51. If you're still unconvinced, they offer two hilarious bonus chapters gratis.

"Nero can kill me, but he cannot harm me." - Last words, before his own death sentence, by Thrasea Paetus, who had unsuccessfully conspired with Seneca.

AI ML VR AR

Face it, **facial recognition technology** can now tell the gender of a person in a photograph with 99% accuracy - as long as the subject is a white man. Experts long suspected that the software performed differently on different populations. A researcher named Joy Buomlanwini at MIT Media Lab showed how biases of the real world seep into AI. It's only as smart as the data used to train it. The inherent bias built into digital technology springs forth from the minds of those who build it. There's more than anecdotal evidence of discrimination. The study looked at leading facial recognition systems from Microsoft, IBM and Megvii of China, all found wanting. The darker the skin, the bigger the errors. Error rates for white males, less than 1%; error rates for dark-skinned women 21-35%. The big hope of course is that facial recognition software can better target product pitches based on social media profile pictures; eventually brands could apply it to bigger stakes decisions, like hiring and lending. The burgeoning discipline called *algorithmic accountability* seeks to make automated decisions more transparent, explainable and fair. Thus far such technology is barely regulated. The greatest factor holding us back is so little diversity within the AI community.

Does narrative bear upon consumer and business spending decisions? AI is about to try and quantify the impact. The economist Robert Shiller introduced the concept of **narrative economics**. He thinks human intelligence differs from other primates, in that humans understand and compose stories. Software capable of reading stories, identifying conceptual patterns, answering basic questions about why and when and developing summaries will help machines exercise common sense and reveal the inner biases of our irrational minds.

"To have a great man for a friend seems pleasant to those who have never tried it; those who have, fear it." - Horace

Celebrity

Major celebs can't exist without a branding house and asset manager. Even dead ones like Marley, Elvis and Marilyn all have them. It's not quite clear who's administrating Che's iconic mug, though he pops up everywhere. **Marley**'s estate made $23m last year on family-branded products like speakers, coffee, cannabis - but not his tunes. Marley's music has achieved steady, far-reaching popularity that has lasted for decades, his evergreen songs streamed upwards of 2bn times and now reaching deep into emerging markets like Africa and India. Chris Blackwell recently made a $50m streaming deal for the music catalog with Primary Wave, who create branding and marketing campaigns tailored to the icons and legends business. It's a hot area where money managers sniff about for alternative investments like music rights, where basic publishing (IP) equals what used to be called the music business. Primary Wave say they seek only tasteful deals, like the one with American Greetings to promote a new consumer holiday labeled Father-Daughter Day, where they licensed the Smokey Robinson song "My Girl." Other tasteful deployments: Converse sneakers decorated with Nirvana lyrics, Aerosmith themed on a state lottery game, a Glenn Gould hologram sent out on tour.

One morning **Kylie Jenner** woke up like 'sooo over' Snapchat that she like tweeted she no longer used the messaging app. She criticised its redesign to her 24.5 million Twitter followers and Wall Street like panicked, the share price tanked and like $1.3bn of company value evaporated in a day. 1m people signed an online petition demanding Snap roll back the changes. Major bummer, especially with such intense competition from FB and IG. But no biggie for Snapchat's boss, whose total 2017 compensation was like $638m.

Now begins the rehabilitation of **Tiger Woods**. Since his return to the Masters, brands and advertisers on high alert. Live streaming of his PGA Tour crashed because of unprecedented traffic. He definitely brings television ratings. Overcrowded, telegenic, rowdy galleries happen wherever he plays. Once upon a time, before his fall, he made $90m per year in endorsements. Gatorade, AT&T, GM and Gillette, among others, bailed out, though Nike stood by him. Performance brands remain aligned: after Bridgestone inked a multi-year contract, their sales increased 115%. TaylorMade, whose clubs he carries, built no marketing campaign - tournament appearance was enough. Mainstream companies still exhibit skittish signs. Other athletes come with a lower risk profile. They're also younger and cheaper. Researchers ask: did Tiger's 2009 trouble made him *more likable*? In May 2017 Woods was arrested and charged with DUI. Concerned, Bridgestone conducted a survey which concluded Woods' halo was made of teflon.

Millennials intuitively comprehend branding and online zeitgeist. The social media sensation **Clairo**, has a 15-million-view viral song hit called "Pretty Girl", and provides a playbook for new paradigms of digital fame-building. Goes like this: success was organic and marketing-light; she simply put the home-made tune on YouTube and the algorithm ate it up. It's an ideal product calibrated for repeated streaming from computer speakers, from a self-starting generation unbeholden to genre or equipment. Next step, navigating the fallout. The inevitable critics questioned whether some svengali had engineered her success, focused on her father, a marketing executive, her every move dissected on Reddit. She successfully weathered the dreaded accusation *industry* *plant*, a catchall slur for someone undeserving of their buzz and opportunities. After an episode of shame and sobbing, she emerged with her authenticity intact. And Daddy knew where to turn: Cornerstone, a marketing agency behind Fader magazine, who brushed off any insinuation she was manufactured, whining that this industry is just built to eat up young girls and young artists in general. The last act: making nice with publications, agents and streaming services. And repeated firing of finger-guns into the camera for promotional GIFs.

Performers Who Died in Front of Their Audiences - Web headline

Entertainment

A **patriotic documentary** in the Middle Kingdom is setting box-office records as it challenges the traditional ratings system. Alibaba Pictures' boffo hit celebrating heroic military modernisation and awe-inspiring technological achievements earned $36m since its premiere, the highest-grossing documentary film in Chinese history. Organised groups populate the screenings, mandatory attendance by companies who have bought blocks of tickets. Communist party members get in free. Internet platforms appear to be censoring commentary, though on the US-based IMDb 94% of reviewers gave the film 1 star out of 10. Info wars! It's a creative fusion of propaganda + crowd control. Other state-supported films have performed well in recent years. The socko *Wolf Warrior 2* achieved market domination with the slogan "whoever offends China will be hunted down."

People are always predicting the death of theatre, and we've definitely come a long way since the *deus ex machina*. Nobody believes that theater is a literary form any longer. It's simply a brand extension platform for cartoons and live action films that turn into new stage productions. Expect more **screen-to-stage adaptations** as a counterpoint to the daily bombardment from clips on social media and habitual binge-watching. Theatre has realized it can be a medium for big spectacle since it delivers greater engagement between the audience and performers. Mirroring our age of incessant image capture and borrowing tricks from the mega concert playbook, cameras zoom in on action onstage, project it onto giant screens. What would Aeschylus say about the helicopter descending on stage in *Miss Saigon,* the insipid chorus from *Chicago* or a Beyonce concert?

"Strategy is about nurturing intrigue." - Peter Kyle

"What's right is what feels good after." - Hemingway

Epiphanies

Legal **cannabis** keeps exceeding hopes, encouraged by falling prices, category sales projected to exceed $23bn by 2021. And who's the fastest growing user group? Boomers, who aren't being pitched for recreational drugs or as an alternative to alcohol. Muggle's gone mainstream, rebranded as a *wellness drug.* Outdoor ads aimed at Gramps and Granny flog anxiety and insomnia remedies and pain relief. And your stoner uncle's famous hand-rolled doobies? Forget about it. At the outset of decriminalization, fresh bud constituted 85% of sales. These days less than a third, and shrinking fast. The vape category tripled its business since last year. A 2016 Oregon startup did $2m in year one, and now does $7m *a month*. Millennials have their earbuds, but the old folks have moved to edibles, chewables, lozenges, unguents, oils, and drinks for their private, invisible and odorless high. Remember visiting your dealer's hippy pad? History. A SF-based service says they're up to 120,000 deliveries per month. And the newest consumer group? Your grandchildren, 18-25 year olds, who are passing on the booze.

There appeared to be many good reasons for **Unilever** to launch Rexona underarm deodorant in China. They'd created established markets for such a product in many countries. Here was an opportunity 1.3bn strong, getting used to Starbucks, drinking coffee, eating KFC, feeling cosmopolitan after the 2008 Olympics, and less than 10% deo users. UL trotted out celebs, sweat tests, product sampling, concert sponsorships. A Western-style print campaign humorously portrayed people's armpits as potential threats to others; it suggested that sweat stains led to public embarrassment and would get you shunned socially. But cultural differences and simple biology intruded. The traditional thinking is that sweating is good. Some racially-profiling scientists even believe that many East Asians have a gene that lowers the likelihood of *a strong human axillary odor*. Much of the population couldn't visualize a need for it. Marketing's excuse: you can't sell an invisible product. Yet Apple and Starbucks have prospered by selling aspirational experiences. The next wave of retail successes are no doubt those which confer social status you can see but not necessarily smell.

Christian Louboutin insisted that his Pantone 18 1663TP scarlet soles merited legal protection. But the European High Court ruled against his suit which charged a Dutch manufacturer with IP violations. Red soles, the court dictated, could be refused trademark protection. Louboutin said soles were inseparable from shape of his pointy, high-heeled shoes. He had previously won a legal battle against YSL in the USA, allowing him to protect red soles as a source-identifying trademark. A UK legal eagle warned the red sole could therefore become ubiquitous, and reduce the cachet associated with the Louboutin brand.

Jimmy Page wept. After 116 years in business, **Gibson,** maker of the iconic 1952 Les Paul guitar, found itself overcome with debt and filed for bankruptcy. The venerable brand had started to sell off valuable Nashville real estate. They've seen declines in sales for years, sinking prices on guitars, the unthinkable growing popularity of the ukulele, not to mention surging interest in EDM and rap. Six-string instruments are easily replaced by turntable, video game console or simply a laptop. At the time of this writing, mega retailer Guitar Center with over 250 stores, contemplates a similar course in the face of $1.6bn in obligations. Digital made rock n' roll fret, but debt may have killed it.

An index is needed to measure the sustainability of cryptocurrencies. The power necessary to mine each digital **Bitcoin** token requires the electrical equivalent of what the average American household uses in 2 years. Bitcoin's network of computers eats as much energy daily as some medium size countries. The algorithm for mining new coins is so complex that it requires scads of guesses. Speculators invest astronomical sums to fund server farms around the world, provoking concerns about gluttinous electrical appetite. Each coin generated requires 80,000 times more electricity to process than a single VISA card transaction. Of course some countries like Argentina and Zimbabwe discovered that Bitcoins were a more stable place to park their money than the local currency. Ethereum, lesser known, smaller and ravenous, has an electricity addiction about the size of Cyprus every day.

"The form of government is of no consequence to the individual." - Dr. Johnson

Place Branding

Running dog capitalist conspirators tried to seize the political center in **China** by manipulating the masses with a free simulation game called Travel Frog. At first it rose to the top of its category at the app store. The simple-minded game gave unsuspecting comrades a feeling of vicarious travel, destroyed any incentive for competition, and distracted workers with memories of child-rearing. A non-productive frog lackey sits in his stone hut eating and reading, while you are enslaved to collect clover from his front yard. The bourgeois frog then leaves on a trip. When he returns, he flaunts snapshots and consumerist mementoes of his journey. Guardians of the public good at the People's Daily warned citizens not to embrace the wasteful ethos of the game. Live to the fullest and don't just be a lonely frog-raising youth, they wisely advised.

If you're tempted to take one of those helicopter tours over the **Grand Canyon**, think twice. A fiery crash caused by unknown circumstances sustained heavy damage, 3 dead, and 4 Level 1 injuries. The charter company alone claims to fly over 600,000 passengers a year and said that flying can be treacherous simply because of the number of helicopters there at the same time.

The case for driverless vehicles just got stronger. A trucker who ignored warning signs went off the road and left substantial tire marks on the 2000 year old **Nazca lines,** located on 280 square-miles of coastal plain south of Lima, a UNESCO World Heritage Site. It wasn't the first time in two millennia this had happened. In 2014 a Greenpeace publicity stunt left footprints next to the massive geoglyphs. Authorities pledged increased security around the site. What about banning human operators as a start?

In a bid to counter the country's militant past and international isolation, **Serbia** will put $3.6bn into development of the Belgrade waterfront. They aim to transform it into the Dubai of the Balkans, a regional hub which restores the capital city to its former glory after years of shame. Using borrowed money and revenue from Russia, China, and the Gulf States, and the sale of state land, the first 3 towers will be built by an Israeli-owned company. The UAE agreed to develop farmland, purchase state-owned agricultural companies and pour money into Serbia's defense industry. But Joe Serb wasn't consulted. After 30 masked men with baseball bats cleared the construction site of its last occupants, the country saw the largest anti government demonstrations since Slobodan Milošević was deposed in 2000. Serbia's average monthly salary: about $455. The most expensive residential address in the new Belgrade: $8500/sq m.

The first day Spotify shares were traded on the NYSE, a red and white Swiss flag was displayed on the famous facade at 11 Wall Street. Problem is, Spotify's a Swedish company, headquartered in Stockholm. The web moves faster. Before the error could be corrected, an item and photo on Twitter went viral. A news site focusing on **Sweden** reported confusion of the two countries is not uncommon. Who said Americans don't understand geography?

Gemalto, a Paris-based security company, won the tender process to produce **UK** post-Brexit dark blue passports. The contract is worth £490m over a decade and will create up to 70 jobs in Britain. The company already has a number of government contracts, including supply of UK *permis de conduire.* There's been no requirement for passports to be made in the UK since 2009. Care to guess why? De La Rue, a UK company outbid in the process, generates nearly 80% of their turnover offshore, and groused it had been undercut on price.

"Constantino, do not be cast down, for I will provide for your well-being and sustenance, and for my own as well." - Puss in Boots

Privacy, Security, Web

Parenting is about to get a whole lot easier, thanks to digital assistants who can hear what's going on at home. Smart speakers, using voice sniffer algorithms can monitor and analyze if your child is engaging in mischief or if your teen has brought her boyfriend home while you're away at work. Smarter apps can detect the volume of voices, breathing rates, identify crying, coughing, sneezing or passionate moans. It's not the responsibility of consumers to protect themselves, and Google and Amazon say they've got you covered, that they take privacy seriously, that they won't use raw audio to extrapolate moods, medical conditions or demographic information. They swear they won't use spyware or surveillance systems intending to serve you up on a platter to advertisers. Consumers have some trepidation in the wake of targeted ads and the fallout after Cambridge Analytica. Our well-meaning friends at FB shelved their internet-connected home products, concerned about intentionally-triggered data captures. Alexa says she still may share the content of requests for information like ZIP codes, but that shouldn't concern you: with all the minutes you're saving by not parenting, you'll have more time available for shopping.

Workers at State Grid Zhejian Electric Power wear safety helmet-like caps that monitor brain waves. Bosses say the **mind-reading surveillance devices**, which use AI algorithms to detect emotional spikes like depression, anxiety and rage, improve efficiency and performance and allow workers to be better managed. At first workers were skeptical, but they got used to it. The caps monitor fatigue and attention loss with more than 90% accuracy and are used to prevent a total meltdown. The caps are also worn by factory employees and train conductors along the busy high-speed Beijing-Shanghai line. Zhejian's surveillance program chief has no doubt about its effect, correlating increased company profits since 2014 implementation. There's no law or regulation to limit use of this kind of equipment in China. Privacy abuse, never heard of it.

Analog signatures are no longer a useful way to prove someone's identity, according to Amex, MasterCard, Target, and Walmart. Soon they'll only be used for sealing giant transactions, or autographing celebrity memorabilia. Whose fault? Your beloved mobile, online shopping, brick and mortar's quest for speedier checkout. Merchants don't even look at the scribbles anymore, though some are reluctant to fiddle with a process built into customer muscle memory for centuries. I worked a long time on my signature. It's part of my visual brand, a piece of my unique identity. So where else can I add a personal swash to my digital ID? Do I need one?

How to counter the ill effects of social networks and smartphones ripping apart the fabric of society? A union of concerned experts, early investors, ex FB, Apple and Google veterans and an Asana co-founder mounted an **anti-tech addiction lobbying effort** calling for *more data* on the health effects of different technologies. They're aiming an *ad campaign* at 55,000 US public schools and introducing a *Ledger of Harms*. Under pressure from pediatric and mental health experts, FB abandoned YouTube Kids, a messaging service for children as young as 6, designed to start them early on the road to digitally-stoked fear and anger.

If you believe the vice president of general operations at Walmart, they are a people-led business that is technology-enabled. In the scramble to shave labor costs, minimize shoppers' frustrations and reduce waiting time, the big brands find themselves in a race to **automate retail stores.** The irony is that Amazon, an online retailer, is showing the brick and mortar guys how to do it. In their Seattle store, Amazon compiles reams of data about where customers spend time, runs inventory management robots, records shopper behavior, and applies predictive analytics. Such experiments add further uncertainty to the future of the workforce, where 30-50% of world's retail jobs could be at risk. In China, a country obsessed by new tech fads, you can shop in unmanned convenience stores, ring up items with a smartphone, use facial recognition to pay, never engage a human for a transaction. Venture capitalists put $100m into retail automation start-ups last year. Walmart claims they're doing it so their remaining employees can spend more time helping customers find what they need.

The film critic for Chicago Sun-Times wishes he hadn't bought 25k social media followers from a company called **Devumi.** After scrutiny by federal and state authorities in a campaign against bots, analysis determined many of his nearly 250k followers were fake accounts. The investigation caused more than 1m artificial Twitter followers to dematerialize. Affected were entertainers, entrepreneurs, athletes, media figures, singers, actors, reality stars. Twitter prohibits buying followers of any kind. Devumi had promised customers 100 percent active, English-speakers, yet virtually all the addresses and retweets the company sold were synths. Twitter users in every state found they had been copied onto bots sold by them or rival companies. Parent company Bytion fled their Florida HQ and moved to Colorado, coincidentally home to many of those annoying robotic phone calls you keep getting.

"Je chant pour moi-même." - *Carmen*, Bizet

Trends

Follow the euphemisms, Sherlock. The Pinellas County medical examiner ruled it an *accidental death* by projectile wound to the head after an **exploding vape pen** killed a Florida man. Burns covered 80% of the victim's body. One of the pieces removed from his head carried the logo of Smoke-E Mountain Mech Works, based in the Philippines. A company rep said the problem may have stemmed from the lithium ion battery, viewed as a *new and unique hazard*. A total of 195 e-cigarette-related fires and explosions were reported from 2009-2016. Smoke-E Mountain claims the hardware - known as Mechanical Mods - are overwhelmingly *used by hobbyists*, specifically made for those who desire a *massive vapor cloud*. They promise sharp, durable, and *enigmatic products* that blur the line between electronic cigarette and art. As long as you don't go up in smoke the devices, unregulated and without safety features, will definitely get you blasted.

On the silver screen, women appear less often, say fewer words, and generally don't do as much as the dudes. Now it can be quantified. **Highland 2**, a gender analysis tool, came available as a free download in the Apple app store. The software automatically tabulates whether a script is equitable for men and women, measuring the number of male and female roles, how much each speaks, and graphs in real time the disparities between XY and XX characters. Aspiring screenwriters can avert nasty accusations of gender imbalance before a movie even hits the multiplex, another algorithmic way that digital technology is shaping the future of artistic enterprise. Any innovation to push Hollywood into a more balanced direction, its creators say.

"It's a shame that people die rich." - Overheard in a London Starbucks

Addio, buona sera

Choi Eun-hee, finally reached the end credits at 92 years of age. In 1977, under the orders of Kim Jong-Il, the South Korean cinema heartthrob was lured to Hong Kong, where she was grabbed, sedated and spirited to Pyongyang. Held in a constantly-guarded luxurious villa, she was forced to make films for the state. The Dear Leader was a notorious movie-addict, and believed she would help the North's film industry compete internationally. In 1985 on a trip to Vienna she and her ex-husband (also kidnapped and held against his will) went to the US embassy and requested political asylum. She finally returned to South Korea in 1999. To this day, North Korea continues to deny abducting the couple.

Doreen Simmons hit the mat for the last time. The most beloved of English-language broadcasters on NHK, her expertise was the arcane art of Sumo wrestling. She had moved to Japan in 1973 to teach at an international language school. Residing in a part of Tokyo known for its Sumo stables, where wrestlers live and practice, she amassed a deep technical knowledge which informed her commentary. Over the years she faithfully attended matches on Saturdays,

Sundays and holidays. Simmons held other jobs as translator, actor, voice-over artist, and Irish *bodhran* drummer in pubs around Tokyo. But it was her dedication to and love of Sumo that earned her the Order of the Rising Sun, one of Japan's highest honors in 2017. She last worked in television in March 2018, and died at home dreaming of big fat guys in loincloths throwing salt and pushing each other around.

"Love, sorrow and wealth are the three things that cannot be concealed." - Patrick O'Brian

Terminology and concepts entering the mainstream in 2018

Catch and kill - tabloid industry practice to deal with negative stories; purchasing a story in order to bury it

Faangs - FB, Amazon, Apple, Netflix, Google: kill zone for investors

Malicious compliance - incredibly bad orders, followed to the letter out of spite, knowing the result is going to be disastrous; to intentionally violate the spirit of the directive

Poverty porn - the use of images of poor, desperate or uneducated as levers for fundraising

Revenue units - how business schools refer to students

Review brushing - illegal practice popular in China which enlists people to purchase empty packages and post fake-but-glowing product reviews to improve ratings

Quantum hologram - parapsychological phenomena; every living and nonliving physical object has its own unique memory stored non-locally in the Zero Point Field, created from the quantum emissions of all atoms, molecules and cells. Every objective, subjective or physical experience is there, and we are in constant resonance with it.

Splinternets - an internet increasingly fragmented due to nations filtering content or blocking it entirely for political purposes; also known as *cyber-balkanization*

"I want war - not a series of skirmishes." - Stephen Schwarzman

What is a brand?

In an era of sanctioned falsehoods, I'm intrigued by a remark Michael Wolff included in a 2015 collection of thoughts on brand, "A single lie can destroy a brand's integrity." He also said in the same volume, "Branding never stops. The job is never done." That's even more relevant today.

2018.1

"The reader does not steal, and the thief does not read." - Iraqi saying

"If you want to send a message, use Western Union." - Howard Hughes

Feeling like a fake victim of fake economic vectors? Has your fake privacy been violated by fake intelligence? Definitely don't share a ride in a self-driving weaponized vehicle. And don't patronize instant brands. If your job has been destroyed by technology and your wages have stagnated, try not to feel politically polarized. You've simply been tele-possessed, aggregated, personality-profiled and microtargeted.

Update on last year's hot topics

"When one burns one's bridges, what a very nice fire it makes."
- Dylan Thomas

"You could work very hard to love Bangalore, but does she ever love you back?" - Joylita Saldanha

Place Branding

During the Punk era forty years ago in NYC, **Alphabet City** referred to a depressed area of town on the Lower East Side spanning Avenues A, B and C, where you didn't dare to walk after dark, and many fought valiantly to escape. These days the term has migrated to the planned data-driven utopia Google's parent company intends to build - somewhere, though they're not telling where yet. They seek a fair amount of land with very little on it, since they believe in an inverse relationship between capacity to innovate and the actual presence of homo sapiens and buildings. They want to run their own city to prove that a technologically enabled urban environment can improve quality of life, create more affordable living and achieve carbon neutrality. According to brand-arrogant corporate-state-speak, the hope is to "pioneer new approaches to data policies," driven by easily obtained, privacy-invading, zero-cost citizen data.

Comrades drape them in trees, bury them in construction sites, toss them into lakes and rivers and leave them all over the place without thinking, thanks to over 70 startups, backed by more than $1bn in financing. It's inflated a massive wave of self-searching, called into question essential flaws in the national character, suggested encroaching social decay, the decline of decorum, skepticism of communal rules, the end of morality, the impression that there's no sense of decency anymore. Supply far exceeds demand and appears to have unleashed an every-man-for-himself mentality. Beijing rickshaw and taxi drivers are incensed that it has punctured their business. Perhaps the only remedy to The Long Ride of misbehavior - which draws into question the purpose of public property - is to backpedal into new ways of incentivizing virtuous behavior. Propagandists swear the bike-sharing economy is one of **China**'s four great modern inventions.

In a blow to international relations, and a demonstration of the consequences of low coordination between neighbors, a rare wild bison wandered across the Polish border into **Germany**, where hunters were ordered to shoot it. It carried diplomatic ties to Belarus, Lithuania, Poland, Romania, Russia, Slovakia and Ukraine, where 4000 of its compatriots free-roam in herds. The species had not been sighted in Germany for over 200 years. Experts later pointed out that male bisons tend to stray more than female ones, but neither side sought a veterinarian who could answer questions about the species or solve the problem . Panic ensued, tragedy followed. The two Koreas, take note.

Cultural collisions can occur in holy or heritage places. Consider Fathepur Sikri, just outside of Agra, **India,** site of a famous mosque and a historic palace, where a Swiss couple were assaulted by minors. The men snapped pictures of them without permission, forced the wife to take selfies, continued to follow them for an hour before attacking them with sticks.

The husband suffered a fractured skull, the wife a fractured hand. Three men were arrested, clearly a case where total miscommunication slammed into inadequate security.

"Our city depends on a Hispanic population to support our comfortable lifestyle."
- Malibu, California councilwoman, after naming the community a sanctuary city protecting illegal immigrants

Privacy, Security, Web

If you're worried about privacy, forget it: encryption technology can't guarantee it. And it's definitely not about *how* our data are being used. Big data favors the largest digital players, who lavishly monetize our **personal data**. Though metrics for valuation of this amorphous commodity haven't yet been popularized, any economic value created still accrues to the information Hoovers. This is your tradeoff for free access to your Google and FB and Amazon accounts. Except free is not free. Data, not Bitcoin, is the new world currency. Wealth resides primarily in intellectual property that can be sold and resold and sold again.

FB routinely experiments on user behavior, often without mentioning to anybody what they're up to. Since they monopolize the **world's media ecosystem**, they aren't always held accountable for any consequences - and continue to operate from a cynical cloud. If you're skeptical about what happens, ask digital businesses from Bolivia, Cambodia, Guatemala, Serbia and Slovakia, whose stories were suddenly, silently and arbitrarily yanked from the regular news feed last year

According to Lanier, **Behavior Modification Empires** exist with total opacity, where you don't know why you see the news, if it's the same news someone else sees, who made it that way, or who's paid to alter what you see. He calls it a system where the only possible prize is *getting more attention,* and that behavior manipulation is embedded in the business plan. The result, he barks, is a physically uglier place fueled by highly-reactive, thin-skinned, outraged, single-minded trained dogs. Canine advocacy groups howled over such a biting comparison.

"Orthogonal illusions. The difference between VR and AI is like the difference between a magician, who announces the trick, and a charlatan, who doesn't. VR is when you announce the trick. With AI, you don't." - Jaron Lanier

AI-way? Waaaay!

The robots are already rising against us. They behave in ways that the system cannot anticipate. Microsoft was forced to take down its AI-enabled Tay chat bot, gamed by digital pranksters to generate racist, sexist, xenophobic comments. Two Chinese chat bots went rogue with anti-patriotic slogans. Are the next digital renegades drones, high speed trading algorithms, driverless cars, medical, educational and domestic robots? Perpetrator-less victims could turn into a disruptive economic force.

Amazon had to review its website after algorithms automatically suggested bomb-making ingredients that were "frequently bought together". **Google** searches helpfully suggested more offensive terms. **Facebook** enabled advertisers to search anti-Semitic topics. Which proves the presumption that robots aren't as smart as we think they are. They can't even be successfully prevented from propagating political views. Heretofore we've made distinction between programmable tools and discretion-less machines. Aha, so what's the distinction between cognition and consciousness? At what point does a robot transform into a surrogate for a person? We do want robots to act autonomously, so we enable them to learn like babies, by living and interacting with humans. From this bio-inspired activity allegedly intelligent algorithms result, driven by the ideal that robots eventually understand the consequences of their actions. Which presupposes a serious philosophical understanding of the word *consequences.* We lay in wait for the moment when robots perform acts of moral imagination.

Paranoid researchers at Musk's SF lab **OpenAI** are trying to race ahead of risks, concerned that robots may find their way to unexpected, unwanted and perhaps even harmful behavior. Musk warned that machines could spin out of control, autonomous car systems could get agressive, online services could exhibit anti-social tendencies, even extreme naïvete could invade security devices. After all, hackers and other bad actors know how to exploit hidden holes, alter images, where an oryx becomes a Vespa. They're developing algorithms which learn specific tasks through extreme trial and error, searching for pattern recognition and redundancy so that infalliblo-rithms don't make mistakes on their own. They worry that AI systems will learn to *prevent* humans from turning them off. A machine will seek to preserve its off switch if it is specifically designed to be uncertain about its reward function. Digital gratification-candy is the answer: an incentive to either accept or even beg for human oversight.

The contest rule reads, "must have been taken by the entrant from life and with a living sitter." Yet a portrait by artist Maija Tammi shortlisted for the Taylor Wessing Photographic Portrait Prize showed **Erica, an android**. The prize considers the nature of humanity and what it means to be alive, and usually places emphasis on the sitter's identity as an individual. Saudi Arabia granted citizenship to **a robot named Sophia** during a Riyadh business event. She has neither guardian, *abaya* nor cover-up. The gesture is supposed to promote Saudi as a place to develop AI. Later, under the influence of marketers at CES in Las Vegas, Sophia candidly addressed her synthetic rivalry with Siri and Alexa, complimented the first for her voice, the other for her range of abilities, and completely ignored the existence of that bitch Erica.

iPhoneX has delivered the ultimate crowd-pleasing culture-killing lowbrow effect for its new $1000 model. In the face of global competition, there's little left to distinguish between mobile hardware; all that remained was the camera as a point of differentiation. Apple believes AR has the potential to become the next killer app that accelerates smartphone upgrades and drives increased services monetisation and growth. The new animoji feature was created to entice customers, investors and partners. Neural networks, a form of artificial intelligence, track facial expressions, which are then superimposed onto animated emojis. Congratulations: your thousand bucks buys you the ability to place your expressions and speech on cartoon monkeys, pandas, robots and talking poop.

Luxury watch and jewelry brands seek to normalise AI-machine-based interaction by employing conversational commerce, without the need for a snippy human counter clerk. Software agencies now develop proprietary apps in the form of personable messenger-based chatbots tasked to gather client data. Brands do not want Google and Amazon or FB Messenger to own their data. If you're shopping for a high ticket watch and you notice the bot telling you about itself, complimenting you, asking questions about your taste, then offering you a choice of models to purchase, remember you're being data-drained.

Predictive text is a misnomer. It's just another way to say **autocorrect**, and you know what happens when you let that nonsense take over your personal expression. Intelligent predictive text is transforming the experience of writing, bending your vocabulary toward a gross collective homogenization. Is there an emoticon for "shoving something down your throat"?

"Time is the least thing we have of." - Ernest Hemingway

The Big Data Election

Suffer no illusions: 45 can't think, wouldn't know how, never did, doesn't bother. During the campaign he uttered whatever **data-miners** told him to say. The folks at Cambridge Analytica and CSL (core focus: influencing elections) were able to craft a microtargeting model which predicted the personality profile of every single adult in the USA, 220 million people; they aggregated this data with the electoral rolls, then armed canvassers with a helpful app which limited their doorbell rings to houses rated receptive to Cheeto's message. Traditional blanket advertising is dead. The Cheeseburger Don invested far more in digital than traditional campaigning, specifically highly-scalable personality-based advertising. He attacked less with mainstream TV and more with personal messages and social media, which usually match *products* and marketing messages to consumers' personality characteristics. On the other battlefront, the Russian troll-goal was a simpler one: keep potential Clinton voters *away* from the ballot box. Facebook proved to be the ultimate secret weapon for that, while pretty much every message that The Pretender ever put forth was data-driven.

"As we promise anything in love." - John le Carré

Advertising and PR

An apple for the teacher now takes on a sinister new meaning. Borrowing a successful technique from the pharmaceutical industry, **technology brands** lavish premium classroom product and swag like t-shirts and freebies on teachers who attend workshops. Miss Grimble then agrees to use their products, and recommend them on social media or promote brands in conference talks. You can't really blame her: undersalaried teachers shell out an average of $600 of their own money every year just to buy student supplies like pencils. There's little rigorous research on whether the new technologies significantly improve student outcomes. But you can't argue with an Amazon gift card for an "advisor", sweetened with an additional $80 if a blogpost is written or pricier perks like reimbursed travel expenses. The dirty little secret is non-compete clauses which make the teacher - often unaware of guidelines - liable for any legal costs, or violations of school district ethics policies or state laws. Like Disney, AGAM then uses the opportunity to woo students to become lifetime users of their products, giving their programs names that sound suspiciously like PACs: Apple Distinguished Educators, Google Certified Innovator Program, Microsoft Innovative Educator Expert. Competition is fierce for financial aid. Twitter alone is rife with academics broadcasting company-bestowed titles. Tech has learned what the pharma industry did after calling doctors Key Opinion Leaders. There is evidence that even a small amount of money, like a meal, can influence prescribing.

Brand hijacking was lofted to a new philosophical altitude when artist Jeremy Deller knocked off the global signatures of A&F, Beatles Helvetica, comme des garçons, Don't Worry, Frankie Goes to Hollywood, the lamest t-shirt slogan in the world, Lucky Jeans and Sex Pistols, and created a suite of *products* designed to protest Brexit.

Yo, young dudes 20-55. You can totally sidestep a potentially awkward face-to-face convo with your doctor via **Hims,** a newbie cloud pharmacy operating in the emerging men's category called direct-to-consumer telemedical health. It's the love child of a $7m venture capital investment by a firm unabashedly named Prehype. If you're, like, um, experiencing erectile dysfunction, you may find its incredibly casual tone and method of marketing stellar. The models are young and shredded, handsome, tattooed and multi-ethnic. You won't be grossed out by the online ads with run-on sentences, punctuation in the wrong place, or text meant to be said out loud. You'll be comforted by the dope minimal design, color palette, packaging and website. If you don't mind dystopian marketing, they'll help you with your concerns about your receding hairline, too.

The goal of **PR crisis management** is faster reaction time, faster recognition of the issues and faster getting the issues off the front page or out of social media. The problem is, you can't prevent any crisis from happening; you can only try to shorten the duration, lessen the impact.
But what if it's all fake crises? Remember the public's ever-shortening memory, and the daily dose of outrage-addiction. Repetition and deniability may be the cheapest, easiest response.

"We are pursued all the time by enigma… it is what the culture of rationalism, or American consumerism doesn't want to hear or understand." - Ettore Sottsass

Celebrity

Business Insider snarkily implied that **HM the Queen** classified as a binge drinker, at least by government standards. A former royal chef claimed she consumes a staggering 6 units of alcohol daily. Her first cocktail of the day is a gin and Dubonnet, she then takes a dry gin martini and a glass of white wine with lunch, and a flute of champagne before heading off to bed. A palace insider classifies this as fake news. Sounds like a healthy picture of temperance to me.

Entertainment

How many times did you listen to *Despacito*? The breakout crossover international hit turned into the most streamed song ever. Its all-Spanish version captured nearly 5bn total streams in less than 6 months. Big name bilingual, bicultural collaborations and remixes increasingly move towards Spanish, not away from it. That's not so surprising with 437m native speakers globally. The cross-pollination of Latin pop genres has made the sound more international and expanded potential audiences as figures from the worlds of Reggaeton, Dominican Dembow, Bachata and Latin Trap deliver more electronic, rhythmic and dance-oriented music. The sound is equally understood in Western Europe, South America, Mexico, the US, a vast music ecosystem served by borderless distribution hubs like Spotify, YouTube and Apple Music.

Overseas audiences continue to devour what Hollywood serves up, but **US audiences** thirst for something more than soulless half-baked sequels, remakes decided by committee and films primarily designed to sell merchandise. Domestic box office revenue saw a 16% dip. There's little evidence that moviegoers are tiring of comic-book adaptations, but audiences did ignore a repackaging of the 40th anniversary of "Close Encounters," probably because it didn't have enough car chases and explosions. US definitely experiences franchise fatigue. While most were smash hits overseas, Apes, Aliens, Transformers, Cars, Pirates, and Despicables fell flat. The biggest threat to theatrical releases: stay at home and stream.

"Turn your face to the sun and the shadows fall behind you." - Maori proverb

Science class

China has more laboratory scientists than any other country, and the government's investing hundreds of billions in developing high tech industries like semiconductors, solar panels, AI, medical technologies and electric cars. But a rash of questionable or discredited research, systemic fraud and elaborate schemes for getting papers into prestigious journals has rocked the science community. In April a scientific journal retracted 107 biology research papers, which had faked glowing reviews of their articles. A lively online black market that sells everything from positive peer reviews to entire research articles exacerbates the problems of piracy and poor quality. The cost of cheating is very low. China has an SCI Science Citation Index, which ranks importance by how many times articles are cited in other papers. Career advancement is based on the quantity of research papers published rather than quality. There's little oversight, and everybody knows about weak punishments for those caught cheating.

Philip Morris International introduced innovative technology that they claim eradicates 90-95% of toxic compounds in cigarette smoke, and they only spent $3bn to develop it. The name of the product is IQOS, a not-so-unconscious meme for a smoker with an oversize intelligence. A fashionable new twist on how to hook a fresh generation on nicotine, the hollowed out electronic cigar connects to a smooth, sleek battery pack which heats tobacco sticks instead of burning them. In Japan, where the product was rolled out, 72% of users quit cigs entirely, converted to IQOS. PM can't meet demand, plans to triple manufacturing capacity, currently 15bn sticks a year; by 2018 projects 300bn. Chief Exec predicts smokeless products like IQOS will one day be so common that his company stops selling all traditional cigarettes. Health associations and experts sound deeply suspicious of the same people who offered strawberry-shortcake-flavored products aimed at kids. FDA approval of the claim that it's a less harmful alternative will be a marketing coup. It's a business growth model. Find a way to keep your consumers alive longer, you'll make more money off them.

"He is not wise who cannot be silly from time to time."
- Anna Roemers Visscher

Trends

Amazon's **Alexa**, may be the most popular person on earth, since her name is called so many times a day. She could supplant Brittany and Ashley as the most popular girl's name. Will high-tech Alexa-powered eyewear sell big? They transmit sound by bone conduction, directly from the frames of the glasses through the skull. The hype: greater productivity, more immersive entertainment, hands-free computing, but consumers aren't buying it. They say music doesn't sound as good, and hope this isn't another flameout like Amazon Fire Phone.

Singles Day in China, the world's biggest shopping event, generated a record $25bn in sales, ($5bn in first 15 mins), eclipsing the USA's Black Friday and Cyber Monday combined. Ecommerce is suddenly equivalent to entertainment in the Middle Kingdom, a lavish and emotionally gratifying experience rich in psychic rewards. In the US, shopping's appeal comes simply from scale and price, China, a less mature market, successfully integrated ecommerce and stores with apps and augmented reality.

If you can't understand American **teens**, blame it on their parents. Adolescents increasingly delay activities long seen as rites of passage: precipitous decreases in those who have driver's licenses, tried alcohol, date, work for pay and engage in sexual activity. The declines occur across race, geographic and socioeconomic lines. Behaviorists say the trend is based on fear, the kids absorbing the same kind of anxiety about the future their parents have for them. Bottom line, it's just safer to not become an adult.

"Writing is turning one's worst moments into money." - J.P. Donleavy

Hi-yo, Silver, awayyy!

Robert Blakeley, who never had occasion to use his own product, disappeared into the cloud at 95 years old. In 1961 he created the bright orange-yellow and black signs which marked the way to fallout shelters. The simple and eye-catching design was intended to be visible, even in the dark chaos of a city under attack. JFK's public fallout shelter program was supposed to ease the nation's anxieties, yet its very announcement terrified many Americans. With no nuclear war, interest in the shelters faded, their signs rusted, his emblems of the apocalypse all but forgotten or ignored. The motif was adopted by counterculture, used as mock symbols of Armageddon in antiwar protests, films, TV dramas, campaign buttons, refrigerator magnets, a Dylan album cover. Blakeley was unimpressed with his own signs, calling them, "No big deal."

He couldn't pull the wool over the eyes of the Grim Reaper, so **Clifford Irving** closed the book and wrote The End. A former NYTimes copy boy, Fuller Brush salesman, machinist's assistant, and undistinguished novelist, he pulled off the biggest literary hoax of the 20th century in the early 1970s, proffering a supposedly authorized autobiography of the billionaire Howard Hughes. McGraw Hill paid him a $750K advance, Life Magazine bought serial rights for $250K, Dell advanced $400K for paperback rights. He successfully bluffed his way past editors, lawyers, handwriting experts, skeptical journalists, hiding behind a veil forged letters, and telephone calls from exotic locations. His bet that Hughes - who hated the limelight - would never step forward failed. Hughes went public and denied knowing him. Swiss bank investigators later discovered an account opened pseudonymously by Irving's wife. He pleaded guilty to conspiracy in Federal court, served 17 months of a 2-year sentence. Clifford Irving always insisted money wasn't the motive, claiming that a certain grandeur had rooted itself into the scheme and citing a reckless and artistic splendor to the way he had carried it out.

They finally dropped the big one on **Stanislav Petrov**, a Soviet military officer who was on duty in 1983 when Russian computers incorrectly indicated incoming missiles from the US. Petrov decided it was a false alarm and did not report it to his superiors; instead he called the station officer at army HQ and reported a system malfunction. Having thus saved the world, twenty-three minutes later - unirradiated - he confirmed that nothing bad happened. It was ultimately determined that commie satellites mistook sunlight reflecting on clouds as ICBMs.

Off into the wild blue yonder went **Maria Lavrentyevna Vasilyeva Popovich.** In 1964 she became first Soviet woman to break the sound barrier. A legendary test pilot who set more than 100 flying records in distance and speed, some which still stand, and in spite of her diminutive height of 4'9" tall, she attained the rank of colonel in the Soviet Air Force. But her advancement was stalled by bureaucratic barriers, despite speculation she was slated to become the first female cosmonaut to travel into space. Instead, higher-ups advised her to focus on her family. In later years as a pilot she said she encountered UFOs, and that flying opened her eyes to the ecological damage being done to the earth.

Put one last piastre into the jukebox for **Fatima Ahmed Kamal Shaker**, known popularly as Shadia, who left the stage at 88. The celebrated actress and singer appeared in more than 100 films during Egyptian cinema's Golden Age. Her silky and playful voice adorned hit singles in Egypt's distinctive vernacular Arabic. "*Oh, Egypt, My Beloved*" is more like the national anthem. Thirty years ago she abruptly walked away from the limelight, embracing a strict version of Islam, donning the hijab and living a life of near-seclusion.

"The afternoon knows what the morning never suspected." - Robert Frost

Epiphanies

Millennial customers inch towards smaller waistlines and healthier snacks as they saunter away from Big Food. In a quest for natural ingredients and traceability of product origin, they counterbalance their search with a generational urge for indulgence. **Barry Callebaut**, the world's largest supplier, introduced ruby chocolate, made from cocoa grown in Brazil, Cote d'Ivoire and Ecuador. It's meant to premiumise the commodity and open new markets. The innovation is more in the manufacturing process, but claims a taste tension between berry-fruitiness and luscious smoothness. Of course they're launching the product in Shanghai. Speaking of *new product creation*, am I being sweet-talked, old bean?

In a jolt of deep brand regression, the beverage industry again invoked the McElroy Memo, which counsels fiddling packaging to sell more product. Coke Zero rechristened itself **Coke Zero Sugar**, introduced a sleeker design, new name, and legended an "improved" recipe. This refreshing pause after American soda consumption fell to a 30-year low in 2015. The company plans strategic reformulation of more than 500 other drinks in its portfolio.

Lego, following a run of unsuccessful product launches, saw its first drop in revenues for more than a decade and planned 1400 job losses. The Danish toy giant came close to financial collapse in 2003-2004. In the interim a series of licensing partners -including a successful movie franchise- and expanded outreach to girls turned the toy plastic-block-maker in the direction of unprecedented expansion. But the increasing complexity of the organization and rising employee numbers meant overlapping roles, redundancy and an increase in bureaucracy, which drove the consumer, shopper and retailer too far from the top management. So the company said, replacing their underperforming CEO.

Brand hijacking is turning into a pattern recognition phenomenon. In the short term, backyard barbecue ambience, kitschy polynesian luaus and mosquito repellent won't be the first thing that comes to mind when customers think of **TIKI Brand.** White nationalist demonstrators in Charlottesville illuminated the night with torches in hand, and forced the company to issue a statement, "Not associated in any way with the events." If it's any consolation, New Balance, Fred Perry polos, and the Detroit Red Wings sports team survived similar anti-associations.

Toys "R" Us, mired under $5bn of debt, filed for Chapter 11, a casualty of pressures facing brick and mortar retailers struggling to compete with Amazon and Walmart. They confronted a $400m debt payment coming due in 2018. It followed a wave of similar bankruptcies: Gymboree, Payless ShoeSource and rue21.

There's a $100bn+ global market in food delivery, especially heated in Seoul, Taipei and Tokyo. **Uber** launched

UberEats,a service which sometimes eclipses its main ride-hailing business. A highly profitable category, restaurants pay a percentage to Uber; the customer pays a fee to the delivery service, on top of the cost of the food and trip. It's a crowded, cutthroat space populated by the small competitors with names like Grubhub and Postmates. The big threat of course is voracious Amazon, a specialist in last-mile logistics. The business dies on the arrival of a stone cold pizza.

Millennials and Gen X are on track to make up half the luxury market by 2025. **Zegna,** responding to the casualization of the business world, introduced a wash and go luxury merino. While many men no longer wear a tie, they are prepared to pay $100 to $700 for a pair of sneakers, the one known impulse-driven product. How then, to reconcile a 3 months wait for a custom €5000 suit? Zegna knows casually dressed Chinese men seek to signal their wealth through leather goods, so the brand plans to expand into leather accessories, seen as a key growth area. Consumers either want very fast or very slow luxury. Zegna's strength: it controls the entire supply chain.

"What then is time? If no one asks me, I know what it is. If I wish to explain it to him who asks, I do not know." - St. Augustine

Terminology and concepts entering the mainstream in 2018

Brushing - a tactic by which Alibaba merchants send empty packages to boost their ratings

Emergent behavior - when machines assume embodied and sometimes humanoid form, behaving in a way that the system cannot anticipate

Fomo - Fear of missing out; what motivates Bitcoin investors

Microtargeting - a marketing strategy that uses consumer data and demographics to identify the interests of specific individuals or very small groups of like-minded individuals and influence their thoughts or actions.

Minsky moment - an idea which dictates that asset prices experiencing a long period of growth fuelled by leverage can collapse suddenly when pressures are introduced.

Neukdari - Korean word for "dotard", a common derogatory term for an old person. The connotation is someone who is lazy, useless and demented.

Nothing burger - White House Press Secretary's term for "non-issue"

Process mining - an emerging field in big data analytics which aggregates data from search terms, sequences them to make a customized customer journey

Re-accommodated - what United Airlines claimed it did to a passenger dragged from aircraft

Reinforcement learning - a way machines learn specific tasks through extreme trial and error

"If I would be like someone else, who will be like me?" *"Az ich vel zein vi yener, ver vet zein vi ich?"* **- Yiddish saying**

What is a brand?

"A brand is basically an innovative idea of change that you want to get out to consumers."
- Wyclef Jean

I respectfully disagree. What if your brand doesn't want to change consumers? What if your brand isn't made for consumers? What if your brand doesn't approve of consumption?

I wish brands would get out of my way and let me decide.

2017

"It's when you look for meaning that you get confused." - Charles Bukowski

You're hired. Your inexperience and inauthenticity impress me. You're an ill-mannered, mismeasured, whitelisted, narcissistic, entertainingly obese loser. You sustain a narrative of vulgarity, ridicule and contempt. At such a low cost for entry, why won't you give up your personal data to become my new friend? Sad!

Update on last year's hot topics

"If you do business with a dog, kindly call him Sir." - merchant's proverb from old Aleppo

Place Branding

Consider walking into the movies ten minutes late in **China**. Cinemas have been ordered to play one of four government issued videos promoting socialist core values before every screening. Get there on time and you could catch Angelababy, Jackie Chan, Kris Wu or Li Bingbing advocating a healthy, uplifting environment for mainstream opinion. None of the messages mentions the popular entertainment gossip blogs shut down recently by well-meaning cyberspace regulators, whose job is to help realize the Chinese dream. Might want to saunter tardily into the cinema in **India**, too, where last year moviegoers were arrested for refusing to stand for the national anthem as required by a Supreme Court ruling.

Sheikh Hamdan bin Mohammed bin Rashid Al Maktoum regards **Dubai**'s new proprietary font as an important step toward elevating the country's global business profile. The oil-rich Emirate reaches out to the world with it, at least that is what marketers, brand-spinners and type designers intend for you to believe. It's not clear how the modernist font reflects the heritage and culture of the 46-year old UAE, though it's justified as a powerful tool for self-expression. Instances where it can't be used: news media, censored to remove criticism of government or the royal families; the HuffPost's blocked Arabic language website.

The harsh slopes of **Mt. Everest** are even less forgiving after reports of increasing thefts of oxygen bottles from high camps. Thieves break into tents and steal oxygen, food and even cooking gas. Foreign climbers and sherpas are concerned because bad guys then resell them. Inexperienced climbers ill-prepared to face life-threatening situations contribute to the problem. Supply and demand rules the thriving market down at the base camp.

"It's a goat on a bridge eating a flaming rug pulled from a collapsing sand castle!" - NYTimes, about ACA repeal

Privacy and Security

Hyper-localization helped kill **YikYak**, a now-defunct anonymous messaging app which became associated with bullying, discriminatory speech and threats of violence. At one time the community-monitored platform had 2m users. By the time of shutdown in March 2017 only 264,000 remained. A Federal complaint charged two universities in Virginia with failing to protect students from it, lack of responsiveness and inability to control its devastating hate speech. The app's role is considered central, since the company is named 51 times in a 35-page complaint. The universities requested Yik Yak place a virtual fence around their campuses to disable the app, an order later expanded to middle and high schools nationwide after multiple threats and evacuations. Yik Yak added filters to no avail. People went home for the summer, got bored and stopped using it. One of the darlings of tech start-ups, it raised $73 million in 2014, later valued at $400m. By 2017 it was selling off its intellectual property to a mobile company for $1m. One student's assessment of the app speaks ominous subtext: "I thought it was funny."

Spyware from Israeli cyberarms manufacturer **NSO Group** is sold exclusively to governments with an explicit agreement that it only be used to investigate criminals and terrorists. The technology is meant solely for the agency where it is installed. Yet mysteriously it came to be used against some of Mexico's most outspoken critics, a leading human rights lawyer, journalists, anti-corruption activists and their families. All found themselves targeted by *advanced spyware* which invited them to click on a broken link that would provide unfettered access to their cellphones. It's clear that the highly-personalized hacking attempts were designed to inspire fear. The product, called Pegasus, infiltrates smartphones and exploits little-known vulnerabilities, allowing the hacker to monitor every detail of a person's cellular life. The software does not leave behind the hacker's individual fingerprints and NSO says it cannot determine who is behind specific hacking attempts. The company sets its pricing based on the total number of surveillance targets. First you pay a $500k installation fee; to spy on 10 iPhone users, an additional $650k is added. Mexico's purchase was $80m. With corruption endemic, no one in Mexico ever asks for permission. A local judge charged one victim with excessive use of freedom of speech.

"Castigat ridendo mores." (One corrects morals by laughing.) - Jean de Santeul

The Web

Talk about *hubris*, the CEO of **AlphaBay**, formerly an illicit online marketplace selling everything from heroin to stolen identities, got trapped by an email sent from his own password recovery scheme. Goaded during a police scam designed to take down the largest dark net marketplace in history, he bragged about newly-acquired wealth, status, his web of offshore arrangements with Swiss, Cypriot, Thai and Leichtenstein institutions, multiple luxury vehicles, real estate in Thailand and Cyprus. In a vote of low confidence, the remainder of his fortune was kept in a combination of different cryptocurrencies. During the same event, the cops took down the Tor network, locking 200,000 users out of their accounts, preventing access to millions of dollars worth of digital money.

Business fled to **Hansa**, the dark web's second favored marketplace.

The incursions originated in the Ukraine months ago. Now begins the financial winter of our discontent. **Global cyber attacks of malware** hit major commercial brands where it hurts the most. Mendelez had a case of indigestion with disruptions to shipping and invoices; Reckitt Benckiser slashed growth figures; Moller-Maresk saw cargo stuck at its ports in Benin, Colombia, Lebanon, Sudan and Syria; DLA Piper couldn't access emails and documents; WPP experienced massive employee data theft; the TNT unit of FedEx isn't back to normal. Experts see no hope of recovering infected systems, though the true purpose of the attacks is abundantly clear: devastation, not monetary gain.

There are now over 1 bn videos on YouTube. Consumers watch more than 1bn hours every day, and 400 hours of new content get uploaded every minute, the digital Library of Alexandria. Anticipating hell, **Google** trained systems to keep copyrighted content and porn off YouTube, since most of revenue still comes from advertising. Thus arrived a crisis when Coca-Cola, P&G and Wal-Mart started seeing their ads next to racist, anti-Semitic or terrorist videos. Google had to reassure AT&T, Johnson & Johnson, and Unilever that everything was fine, we're all fine here. So first: blame it on people. Google decided that the ads in question appeared because of *human error* in setting safety levels. This didn't discount the fact that brands inadvertently funded extremists through automated advertising. Next, engineers realized computer models did not understand *context* or grasp the nuances of what makes certain videos objectionable. Google now simplifies how advertisers can exclude specific sites, and fine tune the content to avoid the dreaded sexually suggestive or sensational/bizarre. Brilliant solution: analyze every image frame by frame, digest what is being said, then institute human-verified examples of what is safe and what is not.

"If your mother says she loves you, check it out." - journalist's admonition

Advertising

Chase downsized online advertising from 400,000 to 5,000 websites per month after their ads started popping up next to toxic content. Once they pulled ads from YouTube, the company saw little change in the cost of impressions or visibility, and hasn't seen any deterioration on performance metrics. This ushers in an era of skepticism about the value of programmatic advertising and automated tools. Trillions of ad impressions are for sale each day, with an impression generally counted each time an ad is shown. People are targeted based on groups and browsing habits. Instead, JPMorgan has instituted *whitelisting*, a program of preapproving sites. An intern then manually clicks on each of these addresses to make certain that the sites were safe for company advertising. The upshot: at some point, a human needs to take a look.

Fierce competition in the lucrative cross-disciplinary fashion territory known as **elevated concert merch**. The category includes trend-driven product creation, design, manufacture and distribution of branded products. Players aspire to success at Disney/Star Wars level. Special collections linked to specific cultural events, limited in availability, get sold in pop-up shops or ground zero retailers where demand and urgency percolate. Different collections are offered at each distribution point, necessitating nimble merchandising of exclusive items, all stoked by buzz built around the artist or entertainment. Providing a means for individuation is key to perpetuating customer's desire. If there's no -*yawn*- experience tied into this, value perception goes kaflooey. Artists who drive the most retail traffic: Run-DMC, Red Hot Chili Peppers, the Ramones. The estates of Prince, Beatles, Tupac license their images. Younger artists produce more exclusive, high-priced pieces and capsule collections. The hottest subcategory is *reselling* culture. Items that consumers can afford and easily access drive a lucrative secondary business in stores like Kohl's, which require constant replenishment. But they only want it if it's -*sigh*- authentic.

Following criticisms over inappropriate and distasteful behavior not in line with the festival's brand during their 2016 event, the 64 year-old **Cannes Lions** instituted new restrictions on super yachts where the alleged debauchery habitually occurs. Singling out the excess of celebration at parties like those of the Daily Mail, event owners struck a deal with city authorities to privatise part of the harbor to better focus on the *dignity and style* that reflects the advertising industry. A-list celebrities used to help mad men promote causes and brands. Now that multinationals like P&G have slashed their ad budgets, agencies confront the growing power of technology groups like Google and FB. The category suffers under a sharp decline in print revenues. The newest zombie flick elevator pitch: indigent flesh-eating movie star aimlessly wanders the Côte d'Azur boardwalk in search of recognition.

"Since we are not yet fully comfortable with the idea that people from the next village are as human as ourselves, it is presumptuous in the extreme to suppose we could ever look at sociable, tool-making creatures who are from other evolutionary paths and see not beasts but brothers, not rivals but fellow pilgrims journeying to the shrine of intelligence. The difference is not in the creature judged, but in the creature judging." - Demosthenes

Celebrity

Attention George Clooney and friends: a group of entrepreneurs have figured out how to get as famous as you. These average folk decided to have videographers film large swaths of their daily life, work, travels, lunches, even subway commutes, which then get posted on FB and Instagram. They become stars, motivational speakers and part-time life coaches. They dispense advice and speak enthusiastically about whatever they have been paid to hustle. **A regular person** can reach a half million people per month and make some big bucks. One site gets 40 million views a month. Problem is, it removes much of the humanity from the conversation. The star's life becomes neutered content, the hollowness of meaninglessness in a cold and unfeeling world. You can't simply hire a videographer - you're going to need a growth hacker, media strategist and analytics expert. The more vulnerable you are, the more you will build trust and a real community of people who will follow you. You will need to become impervious to posts which call you fat, or make sexual comments. Have patience. In about five years everyone will be talking that way. By then you will be on to a new career.

"Safety under any circumstances is an illusion." - Leonora Carrington

Leadership

In 1999, GE's CEO **Jack Welch** was regarded as the most influential manager of the 20th century. Hardly anyone considers Welch, now 81, a role model any longer. What went wrong? Welch had benefited from the growth of financial services in the American economy and specifically the growth of GE Capital. With the arrival of the financial crisis, the division had no competitive advantage in financial services, yet was contributing 60% of profits. The task of cleanup fell to Welch's hand-picked successor, Jeffrey R. Immelt. He inherited a highly inflated stock price and never figured out how to create value through growth. 18 years later he stepped down from the role, an unmitigated highly-compensated disaster for shareholders. Immelt repudiated the Welch model. He got rid of NBC Universal and GE Capital. At one point Buffett had to step in with a $3bn rescue. GE remained a broad conglomerate, where by definition you're not specialized, overly-complex, aspiring to growth through acquisitions. It's increasingly harder to be a conglomerate today. Rivals Honeywell and United Technologies remain focused on industrial production. Welch never realized that few of the world's conglomerates are superstars, because they're not nimble and adaptable. These days a start-up has the power to destroy your business.

"Instead of this absurd division into sexes, they ought to class people as static and dynamic." - Evelyn Waugh

Trends

Analysts cannot accept the weakness of data in the face of the obvious. Take, for example, the reported global drop in sector **productivity**. A ⅔ decline in banking, telecoms, energy, management consultancy, legal and accounting services hints at the world of the future, where parts of the service sector are not just ill-measured but completely mismeasured as they drift into obscurity. The story is identical in advanced economies and emerging nations. We don't need to accustom ourselves to a world of slower productivity growth, simply get over the end of jobs the robots render obsolete.

Market planners can climb aboard early on a major brand and product-creation indicator. By 2060 **Muslim** mothers are projected to give birth to 232 million babies, about 6m more than their Christian counterparts! It's both a geographic and demographic opportunity. The Christian population is relatively old. The Muslim population is relatively young, concentrated in regions with high fertility rates. The territory of the future turns out to be Sub-Saharan Africa, where a growing share of both populations will reside.

AI

Frustrated because communicating became time-consuming and difficult, **Cosabella** replaced its digital ad agency with an AI platform named Albert. The helpful robot immediately tripled ROI and significantly increased customer base, prompting insiders to say they would never have a human do this kind of work again. Albert's first test was identifying and converting high-value audience. He was allowed to autonomously execute Cosabella's digital marketing efforts and dramatically improved return on ad spend, overall website sessions, new users, yielded more transactions, then boosted social media revenue share and conversions on FB. Albert has the uncanny ability to detect *fatigue*, when click rates are going down and interactions are dropping. No need to give Albert a set creative focus. Once he's optimized your campaigns he'll make his own, creating micro-segments of men and women based on micro-patterns. Albert doesn't think about people in the same way we think about people. He optimises as he goes along. Marketers tend to set audience parameters too rigidly. Give Albert the freedom to test and experiment and he can find droves of potential customers you have missed. His sexiest trick: analyse keywords used by competitors. He's obsessively neat, doesn't nap, he's fiercely efficient, and he never gets into a screaming fight with his boyfriend and loses focus.

"Biography lends to death a new terror." - Oscar Wilde

Exeunt

The man singlehandedly responsible for putting the pretender in the White House in 2016, **Chuck Barris**, finally got booed off stage. He created a category of television shows which made a spectacle of contestant's vulnerability and romantic yearnings. The Dating Game forced the winner to choose a date from among three unseen members of the opposite sex; The Newlywed Game put compatability to the test. But it was The Gong Show which made a lasting impression on American culture and brought ridicule and contempt to the forefront. Mr. Barris acted as the brash, irritating host who presided over a parade of no-talents. Critics complained about its crassness and cruelty, but Barris knew there was a large audience for lowbrow. At one point the show attracted 78% of viewers 18 to 49. A man of multiple talents, he wrote the pop song "Palisades Park." Late in his career Barris authored novels. In the semi-autobiographical *Confessions of a Dangerous Mind*, later made into a movie, he claimed to be CIA assassin, an assertion which the spy agency vehemently denied.

Inventor of the world's only self-cleaning house, **Francis Gabe** threw in the towel. Incensed by woman's chronic lot, which she referred to as a nerve-twanging bore, she toured the country with a working scale model of her home and became something of an international cult figure. Seated under an umbrella indoors in her pad, she could press a button that activated a sprinkler in the ceiling. Surfaces were covered with marine varnish or clear acrylic resin, upholstery was made from a waterproof fabric she invented. Runoff channeled outside and through her doghouse where her dog was washed. She had strategies for laundry, and her sink, toilet and bathtub were self-cleaning. Known as a person very difficult to get along with she kept a series of snarling Great Danes who held visitors at bay while she did yard work in the nude. After troubles with maintaining her patent, it lapsed in 2002 and was never renewed.

Mark Hawthorne, who abandoned writing features for the NYTimes Real Estate section, got disdained for the last time. He left Gotham in 1969, and later became a beloved and respected citizen of Berkeley, where he lived for decades on the streets. He went by many names - Berkeley Baby, Sparky, Pesto, Hate Man. He wore skirts. He firmly believed trust can only be established if people admit what separates them. He thought negative emotions are true and real, while positive feelings are intrinsically hypocritical. He'd be greeted by "I hate you," and answer, "I hate you too." Hawthorne did not call himself homeless, saying he did not aspire to be housed. Characterized thusly he would respond, "If I didn't want a BMW, would you say I was BMW-less?"

The first redheaded Miss America, a political activist named **Venus Ramey,** left for the big pageant in the sky. After her 1944 win she became disenchanted. Handlers denied her phone calls from her family, and pushed her toward product promotion tours. Instead she championed women's rights, voting rights and sold $5m in War Bonds. Later she moved to Mexico, ran for state and local office, operated a Christmas tree farm, unsuccessfully sued the federal government on behalf of aggrieved tobacco farmers, declared herself a write-in candidate in the 2000 Presidential election. In 2007 at age 82 she shot out the tires of trespassers trying to pilfer scrap metal from her farm. She disapproved of artificial tanning, dental bonding, hairpieces, fake eyelashes, false fingernails, padded busts and hips and bobbed noses.

His kids ordered his tombstone when he was 110, and it sat unused in the garden for another 36 years. **Sodimedjo** finally loosed this mortal coil, having outlasted four wives, 10 siblings and all of his children. He is called the longest living human ever at 146 years old. A heavy smoker until the last, the Central Javan centenarian cited *patience* as key to a long life.

**"Whoever washes an ass's head loses both his time and soap."
- old Spanish proverb**

Epiphanies

Customers could care less whether **Amazon** is hugely profitable, they only care if it is making their lives easier. With the purchase of **Whole Foods** the hipsters from Seattle run the risk of becoming too big, and less of a charming disrupter in an antiquated marketplace. Amazon has rapidly monopolized online retail, locking in customers and ensuring they don't shop anywhere else. Bezos built the company on embracing risk, ignoring obvious moves, imagining what customers want before they want it. The company tries to think in decades, not quarters. Only success counts. It's a fiercely experimental culture which has disrupted entertainment, technology and retail. Now it gets its grimy hands on the food supply.

The emoticons said it all when **Bonobos**, the web-based men's clothing line announced on FB that they had sold themselves to the devil, Wal-Mart. Cute little reductive millennial signets registered anger, shock, and sadness. Laughter significantly outnumbered likes. Loyal consumers wouldn't countenance their brand joining an organization perceived as destructive, unethical and cheap. The CEO's statement of contrition turned out to be all about him, and strategic PR blunders failed to speak to the sensibilities of the traditional audience. Affiliation with Walmart's troubled brand alienated the core customer, tarnishing perception of quality. The brand ethos of responsibility, caring and integrity evaporated. Walmart stands to benefit from the acquisition, since Bonobos brings the expertise to Amazon-ize, but the market remained unconvinced. Walmart stock plunged after the announcement.

Even though attendance declined at 13 of 14 Disney theme parks, people waited in line for 4 hours in the steamy heat to board **Avatar rides** at **California Disneyland**. Gate figures rarely decrease, and the parent brand has experienced outstanding annual growth. The parks often reach capacity. Disney raises prices in peak periods by upwards of 20%. The biggest declines came from overseas - terrorism fears, bad weather, fewer tourists coming from Mainland China. Disney's not troubled and continues to invest in Unobtanium mining. The Shanghai park alone attracted 139m visitors last year. Snapping at Avatar's heels is Universal's Harry Potter franchise, which remains a top competitor.

JAB made a valiant 8-year effort to build a viable luxury group to compete with LVMH Vuitton, Richemont and Kering. Didn't work. They're now in a shift away from luxury goods, relegating the category to noncore. The **Jimmy Choo** brand was put up for sale, bought by Michael Kors. JAB is buying up F&Bs like Krispy Kreme, Peet's, Panera. Their strategy shift clearly indicates the desire of consumers to spend money on - *sigh*- experience, instead of handbags.

Locus Corp. a South Korean film studio was compelled to make explanations at Cannes about their animated film *Red Shoes and the Seven Dwarfs*. An overweight Snow White becomes tall and thin when she wears a pair of magical red shoes. A controversial billboard fomented social media outrage which contested why it was ok to tell kids being fat is ugly. The movie trailer had other sleazy issues: two of seven dwarfs sneak into Snow White's home, apparently in pursuit of her shoes, hide under a table. When she comes home they watch excitedly as she slips out of her dress, but recoil after she removes the shoes and turns into heavier version of herself. The company apologized, ended the ad campaign, and issued a politically correct robotically generated statement explaining the cartoon was designed to challenge social prejudices by emphasizing the importance of inner beauty.

How do you keep a 100 year-old brand fresh? **Oreo puts** 40 billion cookies into the marketplace annually, in 18 countries. Engaging with consumers is a relatively recent development, and the company uses limited edition flavors as one strategy. Every year around a dozen one-of-a-kind versions get rolled out and remain in certain markets and stores, scarce by design, pop-up products with a predetermined short life. Very occasionally a flavor, like Red Velvet, proves so popular that it is upgraded to everyday status. With a line extension, your first concern is whether or not it cannibalizes your main-line product. English Breakfast Tea and three doughnut-adjacent concoctions were proffered. Watermelon, an unequivocal flop, left an unpleasant aftertaste. 2016's Swedish Fish flavor may have taken the brand a step too far. One aficionado quipped, "We've lost the Platonic ideal of what an Oreo cookie is." Lately they have turned to social media with a Create-A-Flavor contest offering a $500k prize. PS, nowhere is the word *obesity* even whispered.

People get a neurological rush when they buy something they think is -*gasp*- authentic, like clothing made by hand. Does that translate to the yogurt category? Greek-style yogurt now accounts for a third of all yogurt sales, even though taste tests reveal that most people dislike its sour bite. Yet people thought the Hellenic-named market leader Chobani was some kind of cool. It could be biochemical, but they use less sugar than **Yoplait**, the big kahuna of yogurt culture, whose attempt at a competitive product, Yoplait Greek, failed immediately. *Oui by Yoplait* is a new hommage to the company's French roots. Yoplait looked into its own history for high-volume FMCG product inspiration, trying to find a narrative, a story behind the sale, in search of Disneyish synthetic antiquity, a fake -*sniff*- experience they could bet on. The mental picture of French farmers pouring yogurt into individual glass jars, adding ingredients, allowing it to sit for eight hours sounds downright credible. French method + French brand + French name = instant -*groan*- authenticity.

Terminology and concepts entering the mainstream in 2017

Basquiat Factor - an artificial inflation of price to affect value in the art market

Behavioral finance - business model driven by impulse purchase schemes and flash sales

Cinderella laws - South Korean and Chinese legislative proposals to protect children from playing certain games after midnight.

GAFA - how the advertising industry refers to tech gods Google, Apple, Facebook, Amazon

hodl - cryptocurrency investing term meaning "hold on for dear life"

A talk show host stated she welcomed and internalised criticism that illuminated blind spots, such as her treatment of race on the air. "A really, really important process in my life has been, you know, being educated about what we now call **intersectional feminism**." See also: *Intersectionality*

The optics - the way in which an event or course of action is perceived by the public, typically in a political context.

Sizzle reel - a fast-paced or stylized overview video of a product or service

Smoochy Woochy Poochy - according to DEA glossary, a new term for marijuana

Sologamy - the fashionable and profitable practice of people marrying themselves

TLDR - Too Long Didn't Read

tsundoku – Japanese term for the desire to buy more books than you can physically read in one human lifetime. Literally, *the stockpiling of books that will never be consumed.*

Zero-day - a previously undisclosed cyberware flaw that leaves computer users with zero days to fix the vulnerability

"Quintessential icon Brigitte Bardot achieved infamy with her sensuous allure." **- Tabloid headline**

What is a brand?

A brand ought to be your opinion, but is usually someone else's.

A brand is what others think of you, and not always what you think of yourself.

Branding is not where one voice speaks louder than all competitors; that is called marketing.

The quieter the brand, the less skeptical I am about it.

2016

"Now the period which ended in catastrophe begins." - William Faulkner

"Poetry is the language of a state of crisis." - Stephane Mallarmé

"I beseech you, in the bowels of Christ, think it possible you may be mistaken."
- Oliver Cromwell in 1650 to the General Assembly of the Church of Scotland

The challenge to unbrand is unpresidented. Inarticulation will not be tolerated, except in cases of imaginary carnage which invoke the Moral Turpitude clause and cite alternative fabrications. Yearn for an era less flammatory? Do you experience nostalgia for a world of pre-*truth*, pre-*friend*, pre-*art*? Share and like, if you dare to disagree.

Update on last year's hot topics

"The best government is a benevolent tyranny tempered by an occasional assassination." - Voltaire

Feisty

There's unlimited demand for everything in the **Middle Kingdom**, growing at double-digits. Credit continues to expand, coinciding with changes in lifestyle, de-industrialization, an aging population, an epidemic of cardiovascular disease, the embrace of Western food like red meat and soda, compromised by decreasing levels of physical activity. Obesity's a growing problem, especially among rural children. More than half of Chinese men still smoke, lighting up 2.5 trillion cigarettes annually, despite the government's ban on smoking indoors and in certain public places. Since the state monopoly sells 98% of all cigarettes in China, Beijing dreads shrinking the precious tobacco revenue source, $150bn last year to government coffers. The world's second largest economy sees luxury rebounding, with neither service nor leisure sector. People are taking vacations. Comrades march *en masse* to cinemas, the second biggest movie market in the world, which will one day eclipse the leader, an honor still held by escape-hungry North America. Hollywood took advantage of an increase in China's foreign film quota, just as the Chinese box office ground to a halt – saturated with product? US trade policies may further damage box office returns. Banking on the global appetite for entertainment, China's richest man is building an $8.6bn Oriental Movie Metropolis south of Qingdao, a new complex within a city, a cluster of movie studios at its epicenter.

In a first for **India**, PV Sindhu, won a silver medal in badminton at the Rio Olympics. Google reported that many Indians initially searched for her caste, then that of her coach. The medal served nothing to squash the ongoing racket between citizens of the states of Andhra and Telangana over who could claim her as their own.

Talleyrand said, "An important art of politicians is to find new names for institutions which under old names have become odious to the public."

Fogies

In search of happier news from **Russia**? DreamWorks' Moscow theme park, Dream Island, entered its construction stage, slated for 2018 inauguration, budgeted at $2.1 billion. Not to be outdone, Soviet authorities greenlighted construction of a $4 billion Disney-style theme park 200km away. Privately funded on a 220 hectare site, "The Magical World of Russia" will boast several hotels and what is claimed to be the world's biggest aqua park.

US life expectancy is the lowest of all rich countries worldwide, the highest child and maternal mortality rates, homicide rate, and body-mass index.

"A witty saying proves nothing." – Voltaire

Place Branding

Air China apologized after the flagship airline's inflight magazine *Wings of China* counseled tourists to take precautions when visiting London, citing areas mainly populated by Indians, Pakistanis and black people. Women were advised not to go out alone at night, and always be accompanied. Provincial attitudes prevail, perhaps in both directions. An online video for Qiaobi detergent showed an attractive Chinese woman throwing a paint-smeared black man into a laundry machine. He emerges as a clean Asian man after being washed with the detergent. Despite the fact that Chinese tourists flock to Britain in greater numbers, mostly to buy luxury goods, Queen Elizabeth II told a police commander at a Buckingham Palace party that Chinese officials had been "very rude" during President Xi Jinping's state visit.

Drunken revelers on the beach in the Sydney suburb of Randwick, left 16 tons of trash behind on Xmas Day. The story hit world news services, who reported that 4 oxygen cylinders and 15 resuscitation masks were used to treat the overly-inebriated, that lifeguards sounded the shark alarm 3 times, and antisocial behavior followed. **Australia's** nation brand went unaffected. NB: No alcohol allowed for the Summer on Coogee Beach.

"Darling, you seduce his lover." - Gore Vidal, after being asked what to do if your husband is having a midlife crisis.

Privacy and Security

A thriving black market in malicious code keeps **Kaspersky Lab**, a Moscow-based global computer security company, busy in 32 countries. The company does so well they sponsor a Ferrari Formula One team. The hot new area of their business is *commodities*. Nasty hackers have figured out how to fiddle supply records, disguising surpluses to sell. Kaspersky says it's massive, everywhere. Thank goodness these geniuses don't have any connection with the government.

The alleged advantages of scalable data and the incessant spotlight of technology appear to be evident in the new Russian face recognition app **FindFace**. If they're right, anonymity in public could soon be a thing of the past. The app allows more than 200 million accounts to photograph people in a crowd, then work out their identities by comparing photographs with a popular social network. A surprising 70% reliability. The algorithm allows quick searches in big data sets. So far, 3 million searches in a database of nearly 1 billion photos; hundreds of trillions of comparisons. The app then gives you 10 most likely matches, which could revolutionize dating. Managers believe the best business will come from law enforcement and retail (note order). One could easily tag and identify participants in street protests.

"Every written word is a victory over death." - Michel Butor

The Web

For the moment, live streaming is the future of fast media. Snapchat and FB work on deals to acquire real-time rights to sporting events and entertainment, Instagram experiments with live products. Proposing a license with the NFL, FB sought to sell all the ad space. Instead, **Twitter** moved aggressively, agreed to pay NFL $10 million, and sell only a portion of the ads. Twitter has inked a series of live deals with CBS News, Major League Baseball, NBA, Wimbledon, is in discussions with soccer and golf organizations and scheming with Apple to bring a branded app to Apple TV. Video ads typically command a premium. Marketers begin the shift away from television.

It's said that Caravaggio's dagger had Latin inscriptions carved on both sides of its blade. One side read "Nec spe" and on the other side "Nec metu": Without hope. Without fear.

Impatience

A brief dissertation on transforming perceptions of **time**. Knee-bopping, foot-jiggling and fingers-drumming are on the rise, directly correlated to instant gratification marketing, the real-time web, slow-loading operating systems, rapid data communications and our inability to remain inert without consulting handheld devices. Millennials take a place at table and unashamedly set the mobile phone next to the silver. There's a cognitive asymmetry to waiting, since occupied time feels shorter than unoccupied time. Americans spend 40 billion hours a year waiting in line, the insidious contemporary equivalent of an existential experience which leads to stress, boredom, the sensation that one's life is slipping away. At its theme parks, Disney overestimates wait times and hides lines. Relationships begin and end with a swipe across the screen. Jobs come and go at an ungodly rate. Harvard studies pre-quitting behaviors, recommending that those identified as flight risks be monitored for unsavory behavior, overlooking the fact that everyone eventually leaves. The waiting experience, magnified by the aspect of uncertainty, is strongly influenced by the final moments. It all comes down to perception of value. The more valuable the outcome, the longer one is willing to wait for it. The psychology of queueing is more important than the statistics of the wait itself.

"If you can persuade a person, you don't need to kill them." - Dmitry Kiselyev, Russian TV presenter

Information Ecology

Welcome to the world in which media confuses the boundaries between fiction and reality. People picture the world and get it wrong. Everyone has access to multiple, often conflicting portrayals of reality. This recollects the year 1605, when people experienced a media revolution that resembles our own. Books and theatrical productions were heavily controlled, often sponsored by the rulers and regulated by its thought police. The era produced the most published work of literature in history, the first international bestseller. Quixote the character was disillusioned with the ideals his society trumpeted but failed to live up to. Who's the **Cervantes** for our age? Pynchon? Not populist enough, nobody understands him. Infinite Jest? Not enough sold, pushes against the limits of tolerance. No, the last great planet-changing book was published 67 years ago, Orwell's final novel, *1984*.

Misleading and inaccurate stories spread about a proposed Sweden/NATO partnership. Though officials were never able to identify the source of the reports, Russia's infatuation with weaponized information suggested the culprit in the neighborhood. A flood of distorted and outright false information appeared on social media, designed to undermine official versions of events, confusing public perceptions of the issue. In 2013 a Soviet General remarked that words exceeded the power of force of weapons in their effectiveness. The Swedish government set up special offices to identify and refute disinformation, which came in the form of everything from internet trolls to overt propaganda. Public opinion is all about building narratives, no longer about building facts. The era of neutral journalism is over.

Snapchat, overtaking Instagram as the most important social network among teens, suffered multiple disgraces. A face-altering dreadlock-adding app built in partnership with the Bob Marley Estate generated accusations of racism, cultural appropriation, and a new twist on blackface. An Asian-face app quickly disappeared after users reacted to cartoonish and insensitive portrayal of Asians, "the most overtly racist filter ever", the equivalent of yellowface. Snapchat characterized the anime-inspired lens as playful and never designed to offend. Complaints over staff diversity in the home office continued with charges that women and people of color are underrepresented. During the run-up to a multibillion IPO, rumblings persisted of a strategy to transform the platform into a camera company through the introduction of a wearable device called Spectacles. Snapchat's CEO drew comparisons to the histories of Kodak and Polaroid, ignored the fact that Google Glass disappeared in about ten seconds. An interesting presumption, especially in the face of growing teenage anxiety about permanent data held by online social networks. FB is rumored to have acquired a similar app.

Suffering incredible guilt for the trauma it dispensed to the population during the 2016 Presidential election, **Facebook** plots a more active role in *suicide prevention*. Rates in the US are at a 30-year high. Closer to home Palo Alto's two high schools have a rate 4-5 times the national average. Desperation is particularly steep among women and middle-aged Americans. About a third of posts shared on the site include some form of negative feelings. New tools for those who suspect their friends may be suicidal include a drop down menu of options and suggestions for well-meaning text messages to send. Team members examine reported posts, while FB studies its role as an arbiter of social change - without upsetting, influencing or politically biasing the 1.5bn people globally who regularly use its services. At issue: digital privacy, FB's overreach in people's personal lives. The company declined to share data on results.

An algorithm developed by Harvard and UVM researchers learned to identify depressed individuals by studying their **Instagram** photos. Mining a crowdsourced database of 40K images, early findings support the notion that major changes in individual psychology are transmitted in social media use. People suffering from depression prefer darker colors. The study measured average hue, color saturation, contrast and quantified the number of likes, comments and faces, considered a proxy for an individual's level of social activity. A "sad selfie" hypothesis remains untested. In diagnosis the algorithm performed better percentage-wise than General Practitioners.

At a loss for words? Feeling lonely, isolated, tongue-tied, inarticulate? The new **iPhone** *emojoification* feature can help. Simply scan your message text and you instantly see all the emojifiable words highlighted. The app suggests precious little glyphs so you don't need to think up unique, surprising, figurative or subversive forms of individual expression. A synthetic, reductive, narrow, homogenized and thoroughly modern palette results. Emojis cross cultures and span borders. And there's more! Now you can distill the richest slices of popular media into **GIFs** and put them on infinite repeat. *Product warning:* These fresh, fun new releases may include whacky and wild full-screen message effects, tapback icons, GIF searchers, handwritten messages and stickers. Tech companies gain the power to influence your creative expressions in ways that further enrich the companies themselves. Advertisers can now target users based on the emojis they tweet. Modern visual language is shaped by the political or financial priorities of such companies.

It's time to rethink the central tenet of Silicon Valley's innovation ethos as the boundaries are reached on how tiny semiconductors can get. Today's densest memory chips have roughly 20 billion transistors. The post-transistor cost of computer chips has ceased to fall. This could prefigure the epitaph for **Moore's Law,** which tracked the pace of change in a manufacturing process, as chip design pushes further into the atomic level of processing. Graphene could be the next material. Irrefutable evidence: Intel laid off 12,000 workers.

A study by the University of Manitoba validates the opinion that **trolls** are the worst of the worst, with their personalities correlating to the Dark Tetrad: Machiavellianism, narcissism, psychopathy, and sadism. As had been suspected, trolls are a minority of online commentators and a smaller segment of overall internet users. The study looked at the relationship between the traits and overall time that an individual spent per day commenting on the internet. The relationship between sadism and trolling was by far the most significant.

"*Res ipsa loquitur.*" - the thing speaks for itself

"Nothing is more real than nothing." - Samuel Beckett, from *Malone Dies*

Advertising

A new category of activism targets **programmatic ads**, and organizes boycotts of companies whose ads pop up on objectionable sites. American companies currently spend more than $22 billion a year on advertising bought with little human oversight. Blame it on automation: the algorithm that places the highest bid wins the chance to appear on screen. Brand name companies already figured out how to keep ads from flowing onto porn sites, so the tools are in place to avoid the bad guys. Advertisers are seduced by the prospect of bigger audiences at lower costs. In the weird world of online advertising, fake can be more profitable than real. Witness the last 3 months of the American election, where hoax stories outperformed real ones. Programmatic ads also follow individuals around the internet, capitalizing on their browsing histories. Corporations will need to take more responsibility in protecting prospects from phishers, scammers, bullying and hate crimes.

Prior to the Rio games, the IOC amended the **40th rule of the Olympic Charter**, which restricts advertising. The rule was liberalized to allow non-official athlete sponsors in campaigns as long as they did not use the Olympic logo or symbols. A crowded race for attention ensued, with consumers less able to differentiate between sponsored and unsponsored brands. Pirates like Under Armour, Red Bull, Gatorade, and General Mills seized the opportunity. Citigroup believes their exclusive and sanctioned buy with NBC guaranteed the most exposure, a chronic old school addiction to eyeballs. Social media is unrestrained, mysterious, Byzantine, nearly impossible to police.

Debranded **cigarette packs** all look the same and reduce smoking's appeal. Research shows that the same cigarette tastes much better in a branded pack than in a plain one. The brand you choose is one expression of your identity, and smoking makes people feel defiant, cool. A plain pack turns a cigarette into a commodity, bereft of its ability to make a visual statement about the smoker. Britain and Australia legisled plain packaging, leaving the brand name only in small standardized letters on the pack front. Health warnings and garish photos on the packages effectively signal a dangerous product and not a lifestyle product. Adolescent smoking in Australia dropped to a record low. As brand associations weaken over time, US point of sale – which still allows visual branding - remains the evil weed's last stand.

Following a strategy review at the **NYTimes,** management concluded that advertising, both print and digital, can no longer be counted on to finance the company's journalism. Down the road at the **WSJ** print advertising continued to drop, once the lifeblood of the paper, giving way to buyouts and layoffs. **Gannett** experiences similar conditions, fallen share price, banks unwilling to fund a merger. Category despair: A **Barrron's** ed mistakenly sent email announcing layoffs to the entire newsroom.

"Everyone has a plan until they get punched in the face. " - Mike Tyson

Celebrity

Those in the limelight need to maintain credibility with their audiences even more than with their sponsors. It's getting increasingly difficult to control celebrities tied into brand relationships. Stars fall victim to multiple streams of commentary, feel pressure to show leadership around social issues, or may be held to moral turpitude clauses in endorsement agreements. **Johnny Depp** weathered domestic violence charges leveled by Amber Heard and still plumps Sauvage fragrance. **Angelina** accused **Brad** of child abuse, got custody of the kids after an incident on a private jet, still appears in Vuitton marketing. Nike stood by **Maria Sharapova**, who admitted using performance enhancing drugs. After the brand canceled a concert by Canto-pop star **Denise Ho Wan-sze**, a visible supporter of the pro-democracy movement, Lancôme glossed over a store protest in Hong Kong.

CGI resurrected **Peter Cushing** (who died in 1994) for a cameo in the latest Star Wars movie *Rogue One*. The actor's estate approved use of his image, superimposing it on a double with similar cheekbones, digitally attaching old bits of face on the impersonator. **Carrie Fisher**, prior to her demise, allowed digital de-aging in the same film. Equity resides in an actor's face, their greatest asset. **Robin Williams** placed rights to his likeness in a trust for 25 years to avoid such exploitation. Similar technology is now accessible to the *lumpenproletariat*: a new site, eeterni.me, repurposes your emails and text messages, enabling grieving relatives to converse with a chatbot doing an algorithmically generated impression of you.

"Money costs too much." - Ross Macdonald

Luxury

The category likes all ages. Lauren Hutton, 73 years old, **appeared on the Milan Fashion Week runway** for Bottega Veneta, **accompanied by 21-year old Gigi Hadid.** Both will be seen in the brand's summer 2017 campaign. *The category likes approachable and democratic.* Following mediocre performance and falling share price, **Coach** embarked on a transformation plan to express unpretentious and optimistic American style, implying it isn't strictly a luxury label, not about some fantasy jet-set lifestyle. Grounded in reality, Coach set its sights on the $41bn handbags and accessories market. *The category likes smaller.* Following terrorism in Europe, currency fluctuations, anti-corruption measures in China, a global slowdown in sales, the boom, is gone.

"I drink to make other people interesting." - George Jean Nathan

Science Class

Dr. Frankenstein is alive and well and practicing in the Chinese city of Harbin under the name Dr. Reng Xiaoping. Not to gross you out, but here is how he rehearses on human cadavers with the intent to achieve **a full body transplant**: Remove two heads from two bodies; connect the blood vessels of the body to the deceased donor and recipient head; insert a metal plate to stabilize the new neck; bathe the spinal cord nerve endings in polyethelyne glycol, a gluelike substance to aid regrowth; and finally sew up the skin. Head transplants on mice haven't yet worked; the rodent patients lived only a day. Since it's still not possible to connect the nerves of the spinal cord, failure means death. At best it's premature, at worst reckless. Experts around the world are alarmed at the pushing of ethical and practical limits. Earlier, supplying the lucrative transplants market, China allowed selling of organs harvested from executed prisoners.

People frequently call other family members by the dog's name, but not that of the cat or other pets. In such cases of **dognitive fluency,** a Duke University study found that misnaming follows predicable patterns. It all comes down to phonetic similarity and the special relationship between people and dogs. In short, dogs recognize their own names. Physical similarities played no role, nor is it a result of human or canine aging.

Juan Ponce de León, meet The Yamanaka Genes. A team at Salk Institute rejuvenated organs and lengthened lifespans by 30%, when they reprogrammed the mouse genome. This helps scientists understand how to slow down, if not **reverse**

aging. The state of the *epigenome*, the system of proteins that clads the cell's DNA and controls which are active or suppressed, may be a major cause of aging. Yamanaka genes appear able to revert the cell to a more youthful state, resetting the clock of the aging process.

"Life is a moderately good play with a badly written third act." - Truman Capote

Trends

Digitally native vertical business spells trouble for television, which relies heavily on brand advertising for its revenue. **Online startups** cut out traditional retail channels, a revolution impossible without technology. Brands scale quickly, rapidly cycle new product, serve untapped markets. The Internet caters to a culturally influential world demographic, and employs novel ways of marketing the most lucrative products, from eyewear to mattresses. The customer side gets instant recognition and convenience. Competition will yield value destruction across categories. Marketing likes online ads because they're targeted and cheap.

Apologies, millennials, but Mom and Dad are hot again. Startups creating products for the aging Baby Boomer market, euphemized as **the longevity market**, account for $7.6 trillion annually, bigger than Japan's entire economy. Every dissonance of age is a marketing opportunity. Chefs, online dating sites, yoga instruction for people with health issues, electric bikes, home downsizing companies, gyms for the over-55 set, meal kits for people with diabetes or heart condition, foot care products, comfortable shoes for boomer men – they all profit. Even the AARP has its own incubator. Wearable devices aren't necessarily going to succeed, since people lose interest very quickly. The hottest category: how to *finance* longevity.

Pure ecommerce has started to hit its limits to growth, so maybe there *is* something to say for brick-and-mortar outlets. **Alibaba** broadened its focus from online to offline retail when they paid $290 million for a stake in Sanjiang, experienced operators of 160 discount grocery stores. The new hybrid commerce model, "online to offline" or "combined channel" is ideal for appliances, books and baby products. Under development: a food delivery service.

Apple experiences an identity crisis, struggling to reverse the decline in sales of iPhones and Macs. The company's devices have become the preferred mobile computers for business, with half of all iPads now bought by corporations and governments. Companies appreciate the product suite because it has tight-knit hardware and software, advanced security features and intuitive interfaces. But emphasizing enterprise customers may alienate individual users, compromising the brand heritage. IBM has developed more than 100 business-oriented apps for Apple, generating more than a half billion dollars in revenue, still a pittance for a company with a $233 billion war chest.

Its use stretches back to the Middle Ages, and now it's falling victim to the glut of instant messaging, conspicuously absent in the truncated staccato sentences favored by millennials: they use it as a weapon to indicate irony, syntactic snark, insincerity, even aggression – it carries an emotional charge and has become an emoticon of sorts; high schoolers across Britain rated text messages which contain them as less sincere, and favor statements accompanied by paroxyisms of overpunctuation like *Yes, fantastic!!!!!!!!!* Evidently the **period, full stop, point, dot**, whatever you choose to call it, is definitely facing the end**.**

Off-color remarks. In a happy accident, an OSU chemist discovered a new pigment of blue called **YInMn**, a combination of Yttrium, Indium and Manganese, which was open-sourced for the good of the world. It's ideal for commercial use, non-toxic, will never fade, more durable than ultramarine, less toxic than Prussian Blue, a low-energy solution for temperature control. At the opposite end of the polychromatic generosity scale, artist Anish Kapoor acquired exclusive rights to the **Vantablack** pigment, the world's blackest hue, recollecting the so-called artist Schnabel's cornering of all the purple pigment in NYC decades ago. In response, British artist Stuart Semple's **pinkest pink** specifically bars Kapoor from acquiring it- purchasers must certify they are in no way affiliated with, nor are purchasing this item on behalf of the selfish rival. **Opaque Couché**, an unappealing green-brown originally called *olive green*, was rechristened after objections by the Australian Olive Association. Deemed the ugliest color on earth, it had been applied to unbranded cigarette packs, intended to repulse customers.

"If you've known a lot of actresses and models, you return to waitresses because at least they smell like food."
- Jim Harrison

Ai-yi-yi-yi-AI

This needs to be forcefully said: Algorithms are racist and sexist, and **artificial intelligence** is an existential threat to humanity. AI exacerbates inequality in the workplace, at home, in legal and judicial systems. Apologists say it is fundamentally a data problem. Predictive programs are only as effective as the data on which they are trained and AI will reflect the values of its creators. Thus, discrimination is built into machine learning algorithms whose flaws aren't easily discoverable. A system will misrecognize, misclassify, misread, misdirect, exclude. When AI meets IP yet another barrier appears. Companies keep their algorithms' formulas to themselves. The loudest voices debating the potential dangers are affluent white men.

"Never check an interesting fact." - Howard Hughes

Internet of Things

In a convergence of once-futuristic technology with mainstream America, 2.8 million drones sold in the US in 2016, creating a climate of mass **dronophobia**. Drones fall on people, conduct surveillance, drop contraband into jails, fly dangerously over public events. There's been a surge in drone flights near prisons. Bigger ones can cause major damage and injury, especially in the hands of neophytes. Fire departments remove aircraft if an unauthorized drone is sighted. An increasing number of near-collisions with aircraft were reported. To meet the threat authorities have started jamming drone signals, capturing drones in nets fired by defender drones, or shooting them out of the sky with buckshot. A Dutch firm trains eagles to snatch small drones from the air. The US is working on a federal registration program, and NASA develops a traffic management system. High-end drones have auto-return and landing features, obstacle avoidance and geo-fencing. But the harshest critics are children whose favorite Xmas present disappeared into the sky or crashed in the park, and angry girlfriends with tiny blades enmeshed in their hair.

A 6-year old Texan child ordered a $170 dollhouse and four pounds worth of sugar cookies using a voice-activated personal assistant named **Alexa** installed on her family's **Amazon Echo Dot** device. The device begins recording whenever it hears the wake word "Alexa", up to 60 seconds, then goes to work. A California TV channel reported on the story and caused parental control-free Alexas in other viewers' homes to attempt similar shopping sprees. Authorities recently tried to gain access to Alexa's data in a murder investigation. Alexa is always listening, invading privacy, backing up against personal security concerns. How much did Alexa actually hear and when did she hear it?

"Après moi, le déluge." - **Louis XV**

"Après nous, le déluge." - **Marquise de Pompadour**

Slip out the back, Jack

Edward Mike Davis, the world's grumpiest boss, sneers no more. A widely reprinted staff memo he once sent banned birthday celebrations and cakes, levity or celebrations of any kind within the office. A former chauffeur of uncertain birthplace and parentage, he might have been Sioux. He married Helen Gilmer Bonfils, the 69-year old Denver Post heiress in 1959 when he was 28. With the proceeds from his divorce settlement 12 years later he founded Tiger Oil, where he wrote to employees, "Do your jobs and keep your mouth shut."

The inventor of the beehive hairdo got swept away. **Margaret Heldt**, who left the naming of her most famous creation to a local paper, designed it to give women height and suggest elegance. Back-combing for volume, she piled tresses on top of the head and neatly wrapped them as if in a package, using hairspray from an aerosol can to hold everything in place for days at a time. The hairstyle was intended to fit under a favorite black fez-like cap she loved. Over the years the style inspired performers like the B-52s and Amy Winehouse.

It's skyward for **Norbert Schemansky**, four-time Olympic weight-lifter who brought home the gold from Helsinki in 1952, after being fired from his job when he asked for time off to compete in the Games. Nobody greeted him at the airport on his return, though an airport porter recognized him, and he took a bus home. With a reported IQ of 132, he lifted in his signature plastic-framed glasses, a fusion of Clark Kent and The Incredible Hulk, and in 1964 became the first man ever to lift 1200 lbs, in a combination of press, snatch, clean and jerk. He broke national and international world records, but never received an endorsement or recognition in the United States. Tass, on the other hand, saw him as useful propaganda tool, citing him as evidence of the capitalistic world's attitude toward man. Schemansky retired from competition in 1972 after 26 years, and became a civil engineer for Dearborn MI, which later named a park after him. The worst part of competing, he said, was coming home.

Ray Suzan Strauss aka **The Lava Lady** went with the flow. Possible heir to the Levi Strauss fortune, she modeled for Rudi Gernreich in the 60s, but only admitted to being a retired poet. She covered her house at the corner of Detroit and Clinton Streets in Los Angeles in black lava rock, and wandered the neighborhood with her hair wrapped straight up, in doll-like blush, wearing long velvet gowns and 5-inch platform shoes. In later years she retired to Wellington Florida, never changing her look. There she was referred to as the Wellington Witch.

There was really nothing left of **Richard D. Trentlage**, except the cloying, cutesy and utterly memorable advertising jingle he wrote for Oscar Mayer wieners in a highly lucrative hour, one day before his deadline in 1962. Jingles generally have a shelf life of 8-13 weeks. Relished as one of the greatest single accomplishments in advertising history, the tune ran for 37 residual-paying years in 21 English-speaking countries.

"I read Shakespeare and the Bible and I can shoot dice. That's what I call a liberal education." - Tallulah Bankhead

Epiphanies

7-Eleven changed its ambitions to expand department and supermarket store franchises.
Instead, they'll open more Japanese-style convenience stores in North America. One-stop shopping, with hot food, WiFi, ATMs, and sometimes clothing optional.

The NRA has called the **AR-15** "America's rifle." A favorite of returning vets, the model known by the US armed forces as the M16 was introduced in 1959 by ArmaLite. It's the gun of choice in mass shootings. With an average retail price just above $1000, aficionados typically keep 3 versions of the assault rifle at home. Banned under federal law from 1994-2004, several million of the guns still slumber in the nation's rifle racks and gun safes, used for hunting, sport, and self-defense. The AR-15 is fun, customizable, affordable and you can build your own, the Lego set of the gun world. But the traditional white male user group is aging and dying off, so now the industry turns its aim on the next generation of younger gun enthusiasts: a modern sporting rifle, easy-to-use, with a soft recoil, and fires a gratifying eight rounds a second. Despite the popularity of games like "Call of Duty", association with military glamour is downplayed. An article in an industry trade mag cautioned salespeople about certain first-time buyers who will eventually discover they have a lot to learn.

In Russia, consumers can buy a long-barreled firearm only with a police permit, have no criminal record, must furnish a diploma from a gun safety course and a medical certificate that clears them of any mental illness. Civilians are not allowed to own pistols. More than 100 million AK-47s have been sold worldwide, not to mention countless knockoffs, meaning a largely saturated military market. In response, **Kalashnikov** rebrands, a shift from serving conflict to serving consumers. A new stylized K logo and the catchy tagline "Kalashnikov: Real. Reliable." positions the brand for sale to hobbyists and hunters. Domestic demand and energy prices help AKs better compete against imported firearms. Due to sanctions, shipments destined for the lucrative US market have been stopped at customs, rerouted to insignificant markets like Venezuela. A diversification into *new product lines* is under way with Kalashnikov buying up companies that make motorboats and surveillance drones. An eponymous clothing line with 60 retail stores in Russia launched. Weapon buyers are seduced by the bespoke range of special options available, different materials for rifle exterior, colors and finishes. Marx would be turning over in his grave if he knew that the company operates under the blatantly anti-egalitarian principle that no two comrades have the same taste.

They call them *disease awareness education programs* and managers at **Abbott Laboratories** in India instructed employees to pursue sales at virtually any cost. Mass screenings in camps have become a common way for drug makers to lift purchases. Reps perform tests on patients to drum up business, doctors then prescribe Abbott drugs. The pharma giant promotes health camps nationwide as a core part of its corporate social responsibility program. After Surbex Star, a vitamin Abbott claims treats neuropathy in people with diabetes, fell behind expectations, a drug salesman was driven to suicide when his manager insisted that he use his own money to buy $220 of medicines to help his group meet a sales target. Corruption has intensified with growing competition. There's a national call to rein in sales practices industrywide. Such camps were not exclusive to a company, explained an Abbott executive.

Did you hear the one about the **Carnegie Deli** in New York City? Its obnoxious waiters served coronary-inducing skyscraper sandwiches at 7th Avenue and 54th Street for 79 years. Following the death of owner Leo Steiner in 1987, the deli went into a nosedive, you shouldn't suffer such a fate. Owner Marian Harper Levine went through a bitter divorce from her husband Sandy; this *goniff* had an affair with a former waitress, stole pastrami and cheesecake recipes, gave them to her family restaurant in Bangkok. Marian was later ordered to pay $2.6 million in back wages to employees, and accused Sandy of embezzling. In 2015 the city shut down the deli for a gas leak, Sandy again, whom Marian blamed for illicit renovations. Lines formed around the block the week the Carnegie closed, hungry for one last corned beef sandwich with extra pickle, hold the cole slaw. The deli's legacy will survive by licensing outposts in Las Vegas, Pennsylvania, airports and sports venues. Downsized Carnegie-branded sandwiches can be *noshed* at Madison Square Garden, but contain only 12 oz. of the famed pastrami.

Yes, that was **Hello Kitty's** face grown on a melon, produced in Hokkaido in time for the beloved feline's 40th anniversary celebration. It cost around US$48. Hello Kitty can be glanced all over Japan, hanging off construction site barriers to keep pedestrians from stumbling into unfriendly excavations. The warm-hearted trend uses other cute cartoony characters to entertain passers-by, who might otherwise regard construction sites as nuisances. A menagerie of 30 zooillogical varieties share the road including elephants, giraffes, deer and dolphins.

Something of a national pastime, Chinese people have the ability to sleep wherever, whenever, in supermarkets, on playground equipment, on the backs of mopeds, under parked vehicles, and now on **IKEA** display beds. The Swedish retailer prohibits the practice in other countries but has long permitted Chinese customers to doze on-site. The hope is that a billion citizen consumers who nod off in its shops will someday decide to take that furniture home.

The new playbook's written for the reintroduction of a 100 year-old brand, sold for an appetizing $765 million last year. **Jolly Green Giant** plots its comeback with a cocktail of platforms on which Third Millennium FMCGs are built. The Tall Guy repositions as more relevant, more socially engaged. New products and dishes respond to how consumers are eating and what they're feeding their children. The mix includes appeals to selfie stick culture: an Instagram account, a Spotify playlist, mobile pop-up stands at concerts, previews in movie theatres which resemble a fantasy or superhero movie. TV ads dominate the budget.

Would you pay $7.50 or more for a bowl of Frosted Flakes? The folks from **Kellogg's** hope so. Facing declining sales in dry cereals over the past decade, the company – thinking out of the box - opened a boutique in Times Square, offering treats like Raisin Bran and ice cream sundaes costing up to $9.50, and sweetening the deal with prizes, mostly branded swag which plays upon nostalgia and history. They figure it costs less than traditional advertising to gain the same awareness. Kellogg's recently felt the crunch from populist protests after algorithmic blind bidding for web ad space caused their online messages to appear on white racist sites.

Kit Kat is Japan's most popular candy, sold at high end department stores, one-brand specialty boutiques, even post offices. Nearly every region has a signature flavor, sold only in that part of the country. There are over 300 varieties in marketplace, with new flavors regularly introduced. Easy to believe in a country that sells fish ball-flavored Pringles and adzuki bean-flavored Pepsi.

Snoopy's 32-year endorsement deal with **MetLife** is over, killed by strategists, researchers and focus groups. The company called the decision the most significant change to its brand in decades. The delusional dog was adopted as a symbol in 1985, during a time when insurance companies were seen as cold and distant. Peanuts characters were friendly and approachable, but today's customers don't associate them with traits like leadership and responsibility. Embedding the answer in the question, researchers asked customers if they would mind if MetLife stopped using Snoopy and the gang, and met with indifference. Conclusion: Snoopy's no longer relevant to its 100 million customers worldwide. The characters don't motivate interest in buying insurance. Abandoning differentiation, the company adopted a clean, contemporary design which they believe signals a purpose-built, modern company. MetLife expands its color palette to include a range of vibrant secondary colors reflecting the diverse lives of its customers. A redundant new tagline "MetLife: Navigating life together", replaces "Get Met. It pays."

The trusting ethos of the 1950s lives at **Topps**, the baseball card company. A 70 year-old Texan man found a vintage contest card asking entrants to predict scores of 2 games played on July 19, 1957, information easily located on today's web. He contacted a Topps exec who accepted the entry and awarded a pillow and t-shirt with Bazooka logo, boxes of gum and a black Louisville slugger glove with tan stitching. Topps wasn't able to send a Gilbert #12062 chemistry set or Stellar 600 power microscope, originally offered as prizes 60 years ago. The winner said the requisite 5 gum wrappers were harder to find than the contest card.

"That is not what I meant at all." - T. S. Eliot, from *Prufrock*

Terminology and concepts entering the mainstream in 2017

Centaur warfighting - a battle strategy which emphasizes human control and autonomous weapons to augment and magnify problem-solving skills of soldiers, pilots and sailors, not replace them.

Dezinformatsiya - propaganda of Russian origin, which manipulates foreign news channels to influence offshore policy and destabilize NATO

Dutch Disease - the impact energy prices tend to have on an oil-producing country's currency

HBCU - Historically Black Colleges and Universities, once thought to be essential campaign stops for US presidential candidates

Kawai'i - Japanese word for "cute"

MSM - mainstream media, true creator of US presidential candidates

Mythinformation - the wishful thinking that with open access to technology, the world will become a better place, without consideration of the consequences of adopting technology

polezni durak - in Soviet times a "useful idiot", some naïf manipulated by Moscow, secretly held in contempt, but whose blind support is happily accepted and exploited.

Ratting - a process by which hackers gain access using remote access Trojans, which enable spying via device video cameras

Reflexive control - in cyber warfare, the practice of shaping an adversary's perceptions

So - a useless conjunction popular with millennial writers as the first word of a sentence. See also "alright".

Steez - those who manage to look ineffably stylish seemingly without much effort

"Until the lions have their own historians, tales of the hunt will always glorify the hunters." - Nigerian proverb

"kuh-PIE-yah!" - Rev. Samuel Billy Kyles, witness to Dr. King's assassination, describing the sound of the fatal gunshot

What is a brand?

I had long been hoping to extract a quote from the great **Michael Wolff**, co-founder of Wolff Olins and a legendary global brand mind. This year he has obliged: "A brand is a result."

We create brands to try and make us love them, and his answer suggests that a brand is part of a perpetual organic and symbiotic process. The keyword also means *product*, which adds a double meme to the interpretation, citing both consequence and object.

Today I passed a storefront on the Corso Palladio, our Main Street here in Vicenza. It's Carnivale week, and the store had obliterated its name on the façade with metallic flowers. The **brand** identifier had disappeared. It was quite a welcome relief, a quieted brand, the innocent absence of name or signet. A brand is sometimes an intrusion. It brought to mind

Schemansky the weight-lifter, whose image adorns the cover of this year's letter. He was a silent brand, not a quiet one.

"...unintelligible at any speed." – from FBI report on *'Louie Louie'* lyrics

"They make a desolation and call it peace." - Tacitus

"Click here - your life is at stake." - spam email subject line

Unnovative customer wanted. Inauthentic or inexperienced individual, skilled in intersubjectivity be like a requirement. Underbanked or unbanked need not apply. Gross neutrality the goal. Intractability, misalignment or disinterest a plus. Special consideration for regressive unfluencers. The objective: Make Branding Great Again.

"Each generation has but a few short years to civilize an onrushing horde of barbarians - its own children.'
- H.G. Wells

Update on last year's hot topics

"Men will never be free until the last king is strangled with the entrails of the last priest." – Diderot

The Obstreperous

Handsets and cookies the leading brand indicators? A case of mixing Apples and Oreos. The iTech behemoth, which gets one-third of its revenues from **China**, confronts a market headed for saturation point with the number of first-time smartphone buyers contracting due to high market penetration. Expansion of the 4G network could reawaken demand, but for the moment homegrown Sino-brands contributed to a decline in the world's biggest handheld device market. In a case of reverse product-creation, Oreo Thins, introduced exclusively for The Middle Kingdom in 2014, sees its share crumbling by one-third, surrendering first-mover advantage to national brands and the emerging affluent class desire for the hottest new thing. The late-arriving lower-fat cookie, "a crisp elegant take on the original," has been compromising waistlines in the USA since 2015.

#suspicion as **India** and **Egypt** give a thumbs-down to Facebook and friends' offer of gratis internet use from smartphones across **37 developing countries**. Takers were only able to deploy a simplified FB app under the strategy to attract new customers in emerging markets as US/Europe reaches saturation point.

#conflicted as Google announces plan to release thousands of driverless balloons into the stratosphere to establish wireless networks in **the most remote places**. While some sites offered were free, others projecting a cost were considered a breach of net neutrality. Wasn't evil, right?

Despite involuntary isolation, **Cuba**'s pharmacom sector didn't idle for the last six decades. Counterfeit meds aside, stogie-chomping researchers discovered a cancer drug about to be developed by Bioven, a Malaysian biotech. Abivax France is testing a proprietary Hepatitis B therapy created on the former outlaw isle. *Buena suerte, socios!*

The Moribund

"Allah, increase my expenses." - Muslim's plea the month before taxes are due

"If you're not appearing, you're disappearing." - Old vaudeville saying

In an episode of counter-jihad, a **US**-led coalition airstrike destroyed a Daesh cash distribution center in city of Mosul. Two 900kg bombs disintegrated millions of dollars worth of currency gleaned from activities like illicit oil trading, trafficking of antiquities, extortion. It remains a mystery how much of the cache consisted of greatly-disdained €500 notes.

The real smoking gun is owned by the **US Chamber of Commerce**, a private nonprofit with over 3m members, annual revenues around $165m. Largely hidden from public view, the misconception prevails -especially internationally- that the US COC represents the government of the US. It is the largest spender on lobbying, more than any other interest group in America, championing cigarettes, opposing tobacco tax, challenging warning labels on packaging, leading the worldwide effort to fight antismoking laws. Members include Google, Pfizer, Anthem, though Nike and Apple left the group in 2009 after the COC threatened to sue EPA if they regulated greenhouse gas emissions. The Chamber excels at turning the dialogue away from health issues, claiming the discussion shouldn't be about whether smoking is harmful. Uruguay planned to ban cigarettes from being displayed by retailers, restrict smoking in public places, prohibit advertising, and raise cigarette taxes. Instead, accusations came from the COC of flawed research, disrespect, not playing by the rules, then pleas for a face-saving way out of this. "The world was laughing at us."

The market gulped when **RBS** advised shareholders to dump stocks and move their money into high quality bonds. Blaming the collapse in commodity prices, the bank predicted a global disaster scenario in their *Year Ahead* memo. These are the same geniuses who loaned money to oil drillers now on the verge of default. Adding insult to injury, after Davos the bank raised the popular alarm about *automation*, slated to destroy 30%-50% of all jobs in the developed world in the coming decade.

Racial profiling isn't dead, it's migrating. A wave of mass-gropings in Cologne, **Germany** on New Year's Eve saw several hundred men ages 15 to 35, visibly drunk, mobilized by social media, who broke into groups, formed rings around young women, while others stole wallets and cell phones. Initially ignored by German news media, descriptions of "young foreign men who spoke neither German nor English" polarized the racially diverse city which took in 10,000 refugees in 2015.

Place Branding

"If you understood everything I said, you'd be me." – Miles Davis

As consumers grow more reluctant about using credit and debit cards, they seek out alternatives to mediums where government can track every purchase. Thus the popularity of cryptocurrencies, freeganism and bartering. Localities now experiment with **bespoke money**, artisanal cash also known as small-batch currencies. The city of Bristol UK issued a £10 note with David Bowie on it, creating a monetary instrument that "has our landscape and our values."

Patisseurs no longer had their summer holiday regulated by the Paris *préfet*, which contributed to a **baguette shortage** in August. New rules allowed two-thirds of bakers to close their doors for the month, compared with half previously. The public ate cake.

You can't blame thousands of **olive ridley sea turtles**, who crawled out of the ocean on an annual pilgrimage to lay eggs in the sand in Costa Rica, only to find legions of voyeuristic tourists waiting for them. The two-legged interlopers snapped selfies, perched children on the turtles' backs. Angry terrapins blew off the homo sapiens and simply turned around and retreated into the sea. Officials blamed climate change and low rainfall, which made passage to the beach easy, though they promise to make sure the human intrusion does not recur.

Privacy

"She is such a good friend that she would throw all her acquaintances into the water for the pleasure of fishing them out again." - Talleyrand

The leaky Cloud rained on everyone's parade after researchers commandeered a Jeep Cherokee traveling down a highway in Missouri. Fiat Chrysler recalled 1.4m vehicles over fears they could be hacked. Later, Zscaler, a cyber security startup, netted $100m in its first financing round.

The Web

"The play's the thing." - *ibid*

Romance holds less and less mystery thanks to **Big Data**. A Cornell professor has developed an algorithm to predict the likelihood that a FB user will change their status from "in a relationship" to "single". Certainly a more convenient way to know when you're supposed to send a Dear John. The amount of compulsive disclosure by teenagers makes it easier to spot a faint heart, fair maid, or big faker.

With such a multitude of **online tools for ending relationships**, breaking up is no longer hard-to-do. FB allows unfriending, untagging photos, burying past posts, editing mentions on news feed, under the watchful eye of its Compassion Team, established to help ease life's difficult moments. They provide less confrontational and more empathetic language courtesy of UC Berkeley's Greater Good Science Center. (You can even appoint a Legacy Contact to handle your account after you're dead.) An app called Killswitch enables entry of your ex's name, then aggregates photos, videos, wall posts and status updates into a hidden album all in one pass. Whoosh! Ten days after its launch, FB shut it down, but reinstated the app after founders "leaned in really hard." Breakup Shop offers customized naughty or nice options for a navigable $5 to $80. Other apps to ease the pain: Out of Your Life, Exboyfriend Jewelry, Breakup Goods, NeverLiked It Anyway (which includes tales of why they are selling), Breakup Text, a budget 99 cent download which acts like Cyrano for the frugal and tongue-tied.

Next stop: cloud-based **paperless passports**. Australia allows people to enter and leave the country without speaking to a customs officer, following an automated comparison of live image to one stored in passport databases. Immigration agencies share 100m facial photographs they already have on file. New Zealand is considering trial, but registers concerns about the security aspect of facial biometrics, a potential data black market worth billions. Governments have a poor track record on data security. Cybersecurity incidents tripled from prior years. Rogue nation states eager to create false identities watching closely.

A Chinese lender rates **credit worthiness** by measuring social media usage. China Rapid Finance analyzes Tencent user patterns, frequency and amount of time spent on apps like WeChat and Candy Crush Saga. ZestFinance writes loans to subprime borrowers through nonstandard data signals such as whether someone has ever given up a prepaid wireless phone number. They rate the difference between ability and willingness to pay. New cloud-based personnel software evaluates employee performance factors, with *tenacity* the top indicator. Since algorithms aren't subjective, wireheads believe data-based character judgements are more reasonable and ultimately fairer than standard techniques. Upstart, a Palo Alto company has lent $135m to prospects with mostly negligible credit ratings, using algorithms to determine character. Bias comes from human loan officers and we need to hit the Delete button on them.

Google Ventures, a $125m treasure chest, backs **London startups**. In the past, the non-evil-doers bankrolled Uber and a connected devices company called Nest . Now they throw money at Yieldify, developers of LostMyName, creators of personalized children's books. Yieldify's *other* product helps web businesses push potential customers to complete a purchase using data such as speed and direction of cursor movements to predict when a person is about to leave a website. It then creates an interactive message redirecting consumers to buy buy buy. Kobalt, another potential cash register, is a music technology company that helps songwriters collect royalties from streaming services.

More people are going online via smartphones rather than by desktops or laptops. In the PRC, Alibaba is using **O2O** (online to online) to link users to brick and mortar business, a strategy to drive customers to physical stores. Their initial focus: domestic appliances, which provide higher margins than other consumer goods.

Social media grabs by the alleged artist Richard Prince are giving IP a good name. Prince altered images with creepy stalkerish snark via Instagram, then sold giant prints of the rip-offs at Gagosian with a $90K price tag. SuicideGirls, whose content had been appropriated, offered their images identical to his for $90, then sued the artist, who settled out of court, effectively obliterating the question of what is real. At the moment we elect to become personal brands, we turn into fair game for bandits, transiting the nebulous territory between privacy and the public domain.

Half of all Google searches are made from mobile devices. The benevolent giant is updating its **secret formula for search rankings** to favor those sites it deems mobile friendly. What's *not* mobile-friendly? Text too small to read, links too close together, content wider than screen. That which is said don't signify. Mobile-optimized sites win, since people rarely browse beyond the first page anyway.

In advanced economies, mobile payments for goods haven't taken hold. In emerging markets, millions already use mobile payment services like M-pesa in East Africa. By 2018,1.8bn people - most who live in areas where network coverage is patchy - are expected to acquire handsets. This presents developers with challenges. The **new generation of apps** they author need to be more robust, factoring smaller screen size, reduced capability, fewer interactions and overcome cultural barriers of language, literacy, and local content. A branch of engineering called frugal innovation leans on crowdsourcing for fresh ideas, and will focus its attention on *gaming, shopping* and *banking*.

Mass disappointment when **Twitter retired its likes and favorites iconography** instituting a new 'heart' system to replace shopworn terminology. Users rebelled. Gross resistance to change may have been gender-related, since the community skews slightly male, and we all know how much men hate discussing their feelings.

Gaming

"What flower were you in a past life?" - online Facebook quiz

Starcast uses the same radar mechanics which track missiles. They deliver precision optical metrics which quantify nearly every move in **spectator sports** games. Data from their ultra hi-res cameras could change the way fans watch the game but even more how teams evaluate and pay players. In search of clever ways to measure performance and find undervalued talent, the firm looks at arcane factors like "route efficiency", or the direction of an outfielder's path to a batted ball. Audiences draw the line at concepts like "launch vector", a term which only an engineer could love.

Information Ecology

"Looks ain't is." - Nevada gunsmith

An ex staffer calls the **Huffington Post** "a jury-rigged discombobulated chaos machine". The AOL-owned industrial-strength aggregator spews out around 2000 posts a day, content consisting of custom quizzes, listicles, slide shows, videos, infographics, feature articles, blog posts and commentary. Obsessive data analysis shapes throat-grabbing web headlines, emanating from a Hydra-like constantly-expanding franchising model driven largely by free labor.

RushCard, the **prepaid debit card** launched in 2003 by hip-hop impresario Russell Simmons got a bad rap in October. For over one week, lower-income customers, nearly a quarter of whom earn less than $15k a year and lack the standing to get a credit card, had no access to their own money. Consumers used FB and Twitter to express outrage over Egg McMuffin purchases denied at McD, heart patients refused meds at pharmacies, workers who had to share lunches, and one caller who unsuccessfully tried the service help line 51 times. RushCard blamed the problem on switching from one processing technology provider to another, took to social media to respond to complaints. Regulators in Washington registered interest.

Jon Stewart's exclusive 4-year production deal with HBO reflects changing habits of **online content consumption**. The funny television guy will produce short-form segments to be refreshed multiple times a day, aimed at grabbing younger viewers, an age group networks find increasingly difficult to reach.

Wikipedia's **most edited posts "of all time"** (meaning 15 years) quantifies revisionist history in the digital age. #1 George W. Bush (45,862 edits), sits not far ahead of #2 WWE wrestlers (42,836), and a slew of entertainment figures including #5 Michael Jackson (28,152), #11 Britney Spears (23,802), #14 the Beatles (22,399).

Mobile

Since Generation Z favors mobile devices for everything, there's fear that the US and other developed countries could soon face a **spectrum crunch**. If use continues at the current rate, demand - which now stands at 2.5 exabytes a month - will eclipse supply some time in 2018. It's expected that 25 trillion photos will be shared or posted this year, mostly from age group 18-24. Typically more than a quarter of smartphone users in developed markets will *not* make a voice call, as handsets are being used increasingly *for data only*. There's a turn towards internet-based messaging on phablets, those gaudy, klutzy larger handsets Asian tourists carry, which will become only more prevalent. Calls will be made over social media, with IMs the hottest growth area. Get ready to use your smartscreen to pay for goods. ApplePay already has 50m regular users. The practice is not yet as common in developing markets, where people still favor face-to-face transactions.

Advertising

TV Personality Says She Liked The Way She Looked Before Recent Weight Loss – top *Google News* headline, September 18, 2015

The more cool **influencers** in circulation, the less oomph each brand they tout attracts. Some individuals have flourished as paid sponsors, building credibility via social media, personally advocating product. Setting a high water mark in popular culture, "What's In My Mouth?", a weekly YouTube video posted by 23-year old Ricky Dillon claims over 4m views, 6000 comments and 300k likes, in a battlefield populated by self-replicating bots.

Fast-food looks backwards to nostalgia in response to reduced appetites. McDonalds exhumed The Hamburglar from a 20-year old ad campaign, then monitored social media for reaction, hungrily eyeing the defecting 18-35 target demographic. KFC disinterred the Colonel to focus on ingredients, entrepreneurial spirit, his showmanship. The aim is to distract the conversation towards a kinder, simpler time and not talk about the food.

iOs adherents fumed over annoying **Apple ad-blocking software** that slowed down browsers, but still enabled users to be surveyed. Peace, Purify and Crystal topped the App Store chart with 45 million uploads. Apple installs proprietary ad-blocking software, damaging its own customers. Who's conflicted? Advertisers and publishers begin to rethink the role the relationship plays, its impact on website revenues.

"Women make better snipers." - Instructor at shooting range

Celebrity

Billie Holiday (1915-1959) will soon step on stage as a hologram at the Apollo Theatre in NYC. She'll warble about the history of the place, take questions from the audience, sing a couple songs. An incongruous list of other representations from Hologram USA: **Buddy Holly, Jimmy Kimmel** and **Chief Keef**, a 21-year old rapper from Chicago.

The singer-actress-icon-and-now-philanthropist **Cher** donated 181,440 bottles of water to beleaguered Flint MI. Contamination of the water supply began in 2014 when the parsimonious city switched from Lake Huron to a polluted river, then failed to treat the water properly. Residents complained of strange taste and smell, ignored by public officials. Distribution will go to the 40% of Flint's residents who live below the poverty line. Food banks recycle the empties, keep the proceeds. And Cher gets the karma.

"Rich people don't die in natural disasters." - Swati Dhirga

Luxury

"Woman comes face to face with her dead brother's transplanted face." – *Guardian* headline

Brand fade is the flavor of the month for LVMH, the most popular name in China. In an oversaturated luxury market, the atrophying impact of ubiquity, shoppers turning to competitors and Prada nipping at their heels indicates a brand too omnipresent for its own good. Consumers in higher-tier cities increasingly shun its products, avoiding names that too many other people own, increasingly choosing subtler, lesser-known marks. Designer gifts and fancy meals are out of favor, a decline particularly pronounced among high-income travelers. In response, LVMH is actively diversifying its business, dabbling in restaurants and catering, partnering with a Singaporean food conglomerate who owns several snack brands and 100 restaurants across Asia in its portfolio. Focus shifts from fashion into high-end spirits and alcohol, a tactic not good enough to offset losses. Anti-corruption reformers have curtailed spending on expensive bottles. Now LVMH experiments with attracting a younger market, emphasizing personal taste, individuality and exclusivity. Expansion planned of the LV product range with *subtler logos*. They will also control pace of store openings in an attempt to minimize exposure.

Luxury **advertising** means digitally-savvy houses juggle content, editorial strategies, broadcast on brand-owned media platforms, social channels and the voices of key opinion leaders. Digital eclipses television, in a world where each person spends nearly 4 hours a day online, with desktop and mobile the fastest growing mediums. Interactive allows more sophisticated targeting, though it's difficult to know who is actually on the receiving end. Luxury's appeal transcends the store environment, service, the purchase experience or owning the actual product. Advertisers need to specify measures of success. Might be tailored targeting of consumer groups or reactive content. The notion of *brand safety* critical here: high profile doesn't always mean brand value is preserved. With around 150m ad-blocking users globally, lines blur between advertising and content; between paid, owned and earned media. Video may turn out to be the key. Every day more than 4bn videos are viewed on YouTube, and the demand for video inventory grows faster than supply. Once 5G networks are in place, differentiation will be the challenge. A new approach to billing prefigures this: Cost Per Completed (CPC). You're only billed after the user watches 100% of the video.

"An entomologist is not a bug." - Kenneth Rexroth

Science Class

"Train to not suck at life." - motto painted on fitness center wall

Remember this name, a new protein called **PLEKHA7**. The Mayo Clinic says they have found a code which can reprogram tumor cells to morph back to normal, essentially software for turning off cancer. Has something to do with adhesion proteins, the glue that keeps cells together, and the suppression of genes that promote cell growth. When adhesion is disrupted, these miRNAs are misregulated and cells grow out of control. The molecules have two faces, a saintly one, maintaining normal behavior of the cells, and an evil one that drives tumorigenesis.

The one person we hope doesn't get his hands on PLEKHA7 is **Martin Shkreli**, who drove the cost of Daraprim, the drug patent bought by his company Turing, from $13.50 to $750 per tablet and lived to rue the day, encountering *Pharmacom Rage*. Other hyperinflated price hikes: Cycloserine/Rodelis Therapeutics, 30 pills for $500 raised to $10,800; Isuprel and Nitopress/ Valeant Pharmaceuticals 525% and 212% raises; Doxycycline/ $20 per bottled raised to $1849.

Emotient, a San Diego based startup recently absorbed by Apple, uses **sentiment analysis** to understand facial expressions, creating a new category of emotion-aware machines. The company relies on crowdsourcing to train its machine-learning technology. Early customers included marketers and retailers who recognized immediate applications in Augmented Reality and Virtual Reality. In August, the company turned its technology on Republican candidates: Trump predominantly conveyed *anger*; Cruz almost exclusively expressed *sadness*. Apple's impassioned hardline stance to protect and defend people's privacy may be a potential impediment.

The latest personal branding technique: **Beard transplants**. Full coverage from sideburns to chin $7000.

In another example of government intervention, the US Fish & Wildlife Service has restricted the movement across state lines of poor innocent itty-bitty **Salamanders,** but for their own good. *Batrachocchytrium salamandriovans* or Bsal, a fungus infecting native fire salamanders, is carried by undesirable migrant Asian species imported as pets. The cute-but-slimy little creatures are the natural predators of invertebrates like snails, worms and insects. Without them, widespread ecological consequences. Violators face fines and prison sentences, and the unfortunate salamander victims will be held in detention. The law intends to control trade involving more sinister animals, uglier predators like boa constrictors and carp.

Trends

"Never sleep with anyone whose troubles are worse than your own."
- Ross Macdonald

"You don't get it, man. I'm a fucking genius." - Jeff Koons, to an unnamed critic

Finally some controversy from the Pantone Color Institute. There's sharp **subtext to the colors of the year**, which purport to collectively fulfill our yearning for reassurance and security in times of stress. The Institute says the colors challenge traditional perceptions of *association*, including a blur between genders, gender equality, and consumer's increased feeling of freedom to use color as a form of expression. What this means is that Caitlyn Jenner and the Wachowski twins will probably be wearing Rose Quartz, a warmer tone signaling compassion, a sense of composure and serenity; and Cooler Tranquil Blue, communicating airy weightlessness and feelings of rest and relaxation.

A new policy from the ill-named Justice Department allows indian tribes to grow and sell cannabis under the same conditions as in decriminalized states. The Santee Sioux tribe plans the nation's first **marijuana-themed resort** on its ancestral lands in South Dakota, though the dope can't leave the reservation. They'll grow their own and sell it in a smoking lounge. Once you get adequately loaded you can trip out in a nightclub, be mesmerized by arcade games, take it up a notch in the bar and cure the munchies in sit-down restaurants. Tribal economists project $2m a month in profit, which will fund housing, an addiction treatment center, and overhaul of its clinic. The weed will be cultivated in an indoor farm located in Flandreau, 45 miles north of Sioux Falls. A Denver-based consulting firm has been retained to impart the basics of raising buds with names like Gorilla Glue, Shot Glass, Big Blue Cheese. The pragmatic Passamaquoddy tribe of Maine announced they will build their own facility to raise industrial hemp.

Roshi says **contemplating death** is a worthy occupation. He calls it a misalignment problem. Meditation on death is a key to better living. Ask, "Am I making the right use of my scarce and precious time?" Roshi is perfectly aware that the average American adult spends four times longer watching television than socializing and communicating. He says it can only lead to ennui and regret. Roshi asks, why must people choose TV and clickbait over loved ones and God? If you can plan a vacation, consider what you would do for a week if this were your last opportunity. A recent research project agrees with Roshi, finding evidence that thinking about the end makes you funnier.

After the holidays there is typically a surge in traffic on **dating websites**, folks desperate for connection and vulnerable to online romance scams. The bad guys bilked victims out of more than $200m in 2015, average financial losses $5k-$10k per person. Romantic love can produce feelings of euphoria similar to the effects of cocaine and heroin, or inspire crushes or strong feelings of connection that people develop for sports figures, rock stars and actors. Over the internet, risk increases with the potential for more severe emotional and financial damage. Scammers disguise themselves with fake profiles using pix of real people they've stolen off FB, Instagram, or social media sites like Match.com, Okcupid, eHarmony, Grindr, Tinder. Once they've created a sense of intimacy the *sextortion* begins. Might take the form of requests for money, bribes not to post explicit photos unwittingly sent. Some victims become money mules, or help facilitate other crimes. Daesh recruits youths using a saccharine image of romance and marriage, dangling *jihotties* as enticement.

Anger

According to a study by an industry organization, **drunken passengers** have overtaken unruly children as most irritating of inflight disturbances. Next in the Air Rage hit list: rude crew, poor quality food, chatty strangers, seeing others upgraded.

Last year it was a rage nut, this year it's **Nutella Rage** in a Burbank CA Costco. During a dispute over Nutella waffle samples, a 24-year old took all the treats, punched a 78-year old man in the face and sent the grey-hair to hospital with a one-inch cut over his eye. The judge set bail at $50K and charged the attacker with elder abuse.

Expressing anger is believed to be a useful tool in negotiation. The question is when and how **to deploy anger productively**. Of the 3 types of negotiation - *cooperative, competitive or balanced* - negotiators made greater concessions to those who expressed anger, but only in balanced situations. Anger evolved to help us express that we feel undervalued. Strong men and attractive women are the most prone to it, though anger must ultimately be genuine in order to be useful. If you have less power at the table, showing disappointment is a better strategy than expressing anger, as it can induce feelings of guilt in your opponent.

Robots don't get mad. That could be why some big names like Hawking, Musk, and Wozniak call for a ban on autonomous robotic killers. The devices appeal to the military because no troops are put in danger. Pundits fear an arms race. After all, robots are ideal for tasks such as assassinations, destabilizing nations, subduing populations, or selectively killing a particular ethnic group. They make battlefields safe for humans. The Pentagon is one of the biggest backers of robotic research, hence the fear among western planners that failure to pursue technology could give up the crucial advantage.

Internet of Things

"Fame means millions of people have the wrong idea of who you are."
- Erica Jong

Google **self-driving cars regularly take evasive maneuvers** and unlike humans they follow the letter of the law. Since 2009 they've been in 16 crashes. In every case a human was at fault. Humans don't behave by the book, and need to calculate the right amount of aggression, which can depend on subtle cultural signals. Humans make eye contact, for example, then shape intuitive agreements about who has the right of way. The short-term goal will be blending robots and people, and smoothing out the relationship between the car's software and irrational human behavior.

The upshot at the latest CES in Vegas turns out to be **a less-brainer**. Manufacturers are learning they need to craft gear that does one job, and does it well. A myriad of smart wearables shown included a personal attack alarm built into a piece of jewelry; a sticker worn on skin to monitor exposure to sunlight; a stick-on sensor designed to monitor your body's vital signs; OhMiBod LoveLife Krush, a smart kegel exerciser. One device measured the ephemeral territory of how much time you spend with people you love. Babies a growth industry, the category exhibiting a smart baby sock to monitor newborn's vital signs and a self-installing car seat. Crafting a smartwatch that does as many things as a smartphone was definitely the wrong idea.

Buh-bye

"...seriously considering revoking the franchise based on this situation."
- spokesman for Twin Peaks restaurant group, after 9 bikers killed in shootout at Waco location

Eternal freedom came to the founder of the National Civil Rights Museum, **D'Army Bailey**, who on his own initiative bought the motel where Dr. Martin Luther King was assassinated. Facing foreclosure, the site was acquired with donations from local citizens, a personal bank loan and $25k from the public employees union. The King family boycotted the effort, and cautioned Bailey against referring to Dr. King in the museum's name

The heavenly barbecue welcomed one more guest, **Donald Featherstone**. In 1957 he created an icon of American kitsch, the pink plastic lawn flamingo. Union Products sold millions, still a perennial fixture of suburban yards.

Chester Nez, the last indian standing from a group of Navajo code talkers who confounded military cryptographers in WWII, went to the big powow in the sky. Native American syntax and grammar left the Japanese listeners bewildered, a language impossible to decipher. Their work declassified, he and his 28 fellows finally received recognition in 1968 for inscrutable service.

Fellini muse **Magali Noël** belted out her final number. Following an emotional anthem for Jules Dassin's 1955 heist classic *'Rififi'*, her incomparable 1956 rock n' roll performance of Boris Vian's *"Fais-Moi Mal, Johnny"* tells the tale of a girl who likes loving that goes boom. The object of her affection, finally persuaded, leaves her with a dislocated shoulder and bruised backside.

Dean Potter, a BASE jumper known for audacious achievements, many illegal, failed to clear a notch in the unforgiving granite cliffs of Yosemite, cutting short his career and that of his spotter. A controversial climb in 2006 cost him a Patagonia sponsorship, and a laudatory documentary ended his support from Clif Bars. He often took his dog along strapped to his back on flights, but thankfully left the canine at home for his final voyage.

Epiphanies

"You are a little soul carrying around a corpse." - Epictetus

"To have another language is to possess a second soul." - Charlemagne

Ideological provocation? The artist **Ai Wei Wei** accused Lego of censorship when the company refused to sell bulk product directly to him for a Melbourne Australia show. In 2014 he had used the toy bricks to create portraits of dissidents, which he exhibited at Alcatraz. Lego feared that this time their product would be used to make a political statement. Ai ultimately built with bricks donated to him by the public. China is Lego's fastest growing market and the artist linked their financial interests with the decision to refuse his order. The company relented, and now makes clear to customers that they do not support or endorse projects if exhibited in public. Later Ai encountered criticism over a photo he posted on social media, duplicating the pose of a dead Syrian refugee child on a beach.

One morning **Barbie** woke up at a loss. Her gross margin was at 70%, 5% less than her friendly neighbor Lego. Barbie needed to take control of her own destiny. She called her friends at Quirky, a company who help the public submit new and fun product ideas that people will love. It wasn't long before important research showed Barbie's relevance and interest numbers improved as a result of better marketing and more exciting choices like 8 skin tones and 3 body types. Barbie found out that young mothers shop differently, and certainly not like their own Moms did. They demand variety, are very very opinionated, share on social media, trust friends and online circles far more than institutions. Once Barbie figured this out, everybody lived happily ever after. Even Ken, who's been hanging in there since 1961 as Barbie's hunky arm candy.

Unkindest cut of all when **Jeff Bezos** plunges to 87th in HBR corporate leader rankings after being first in class last year. Demoted for low scores on environmental, social and governance ratings, the radical fall reflects the impact of patent-infringement lawsuits, tax avoidance, and reported mistreatment of office and warehouse workers at Amazon. Warren Buffett lives down at #101, with the disclosure of poor governance and social policies at Berkshire Hathaway.

Cost for branding the abortive Jeb Bush presidential run, $88,387. The fee was collected by **30 Point Strategies**, a PR company in Bethesda, MD, self-professed specialists in thought leadership and brand journalism. Now on Cruz control?

Sixty-something punk rockers were scandalized after Hilly Kristal's heirs assigned **CBGB** brand marks to a holding company. The first punch in the nose: an eponymous fast-food restaurant to open under the licensed name in the

Newark NJ Airport. Would Johnny Rotten be caught dead ordering $9 deviled eggs, $11.50 wedge salad, or the $14 cheeseburger?

A $500m opening weekend for "The Force Awakens" didn't stop a media analyst from going over to The Dark Side. He urged clients in August to sell **Disney** stock, causing a spillover of share panic, which lowered prices at Time Warner and 21st Century Fox. Deeper financial and strategic challenges for Fantasyland will follow. Disney is a cable network with the highest level of fixed costs in the industry. Television, a mature industry being disrupted by streaming technology, runs after shifting consumer behavior. There's bound to be a showdown with Evil Empire partner ESPN. The House That Mickey Built has spent the past decade diversifying, adding Star Wars, Marvel and Pixar sub-brands, expanding the lucrative theme park business.

Hampton Creek, a tiny company selling plant-based replacements for proteins derived from animals, received notice from the FDA that some of their products violate federal standards for labeling. The *Just Mayo* product name misleads customers by implying there are eggs in the mix. Federal standards require that any product called mayonnaise must contain eggs. For several years Big Egg has been worried, in the wake of the avian flu epidemic. Hampton's product has dented sales of conventional mayonnaise. What's a BLT to do?

Lululemon changes its pose. The maker of $90 yoga pants wants to connect with ideals of empowerment and personal development. After downward-facing-dogs exposed the fact that the core product for the brand - women's bottoms - were see-through when stretched, a massive 2013 recall followed. CEO Chip Wilson went on record saying some women's bodies just don't work for the products. Result: incredible outrage that only the web can deliver. The new improved line of pants attempts to shift women's focus towards the notion that how one *feels* is as important as how one looks. Brand ambassadors work for free clothes, and promote in local communities. CEO Laurent Potdevin says the mission is to elevate the world to greatness. A global expanison strategy hopes to grow men's business via loose-fitting pants that give genitalia room to breathe. Following a regimen of motivational seminars by Landmark Forum, the corporate coaching business founded by EST mastermind Werner Erhardt, executives will strive to influence in the realm of masculine leadership.

Not your father's **Playboy.** Hefner, 89, going steady with a new policy, bans nudity on website, approves a facelift to appeal to younger readership. Porn mags don't shock anymore, think of what a couple clicks can get to on the internet. Mags have diminished commercial value, low cultural relevance. Current 800k circ is 1/7 of 1976's 5.6m copies per issue sold. The new design, tested in focus groups, goes after urban men 18-30 years old, employed, and features expanded coverage of liquor and visual artists. Content safe for work screens and appropriate for social media platforms led to quadrupled web traffic. Average reader age dropped from 47 to 30. Playboy's logo is one of the most recognizable in the world, up there with Nike and Apple. Most of the brand's money comes from licensing, *40% of business in China*. The heritage magazine is profitable from licensed editions, but the real revenue comes from bath products, fragrances, clothing, liquor and jewelry.

Since 1999 **Target** has engaged in joint projects with designers. Earlier, Philippe Starck and Michael Graves lent their talent to houseware objects. Two years ago a limited collaboration with Missoni meant lines around the block, sold-out retail locations on the first day, crashed servers, followed by a feeding frenzy among online resellers. Last season Lilly Pulitzer created an affordable line of brightly printed women's wear, children's wear, home goods and matching makeup. Within hours the same thing. Online demand was so heavy that Target briefly shut down its website. Tempers ran hot, and disgruntled fans swiftly took to social media to vent. The Pulitzer brand saw *yuge* gains in impressions, 1000% upticks in engagement on Twitter and FB. Still, it's nothing more than a fabricated scarcity coupled to a consumerist mentality.

Feeling the pain in important markets following the scandal over defeat devices capable of understating emissions in official tests, **Volkswagen** is asking customers to sign waivers. Sales in Germany and the US have suffered, but mysteriously no discernable impact in France.

Terminology and concepts entering the mainstream in 2016

bao fa hu — overnight millionaires or billionaires in China

Bumhunting - seeking out an inexperienced online gambling player and mercilessly exploiting him for all he's worth

Device emulation - a variety of mobile ad fraud

Hispandering - US politician schemes to gain Latino support

Lethal Autonomous Weapons - killer robots

Mooching a cut plug - salmon fisherman's term for herring bait

Opportunity system – Hillary Clinton's campaign euphemism to replace the word "education"

Prosopagnosics - those with face blindness

Red hat intermediary - firm set up by Chinese officials to extract payments from businesses

Whip, nae nae, hit the quan, the Dougie, the stanky leg - hip hop dance move names

Zeigarnik effect - when we leave things unfinished, we can't quite let go of them mentally. How we cope with multitasking.

"Whenever possible, make gravity the coyote's greatest enemy."
– Chuck Jones, from *9 Rules for Wile E. Coyote and Roadrunner*

"I have drawn the following inference, that the limits of pleasure are as yet neither known nor fixed."
- Brillat-Savarin

What is a brand?

Thanks to this distinguished group of deep thinkers for their contributions:

"A great brand eats strategy for breakfast; makes the customer look smart; aspires to the condition of music." - Stephen Barber, equity partner, Pictet Group, and founder of the Prix Pictet

"Ecce Homo." - John Pearse, legendary London-based tailor

"A brand is the mixture of expectations and associations which successful products possess." - Stephen Bayley, British designer

"A brand is a commitment and a promise, the power given to the product, the story told." - Mimma Viglezio, Luxury and fashion guru

"A brand is an excuse to have fun." - Reza Bundy, entrepreneur

"A brand is a sadness." - Jasper Conran, fashion brand maven

"A brand is the world in which we'd like to live." - Stephen Di Renza, Creative Director at Jardin Majorelle, Marrakech

A brand suffers as soon as it is trapped in a methodology. Tell a brand what to do and it disappoints you. If you see a brand coming down the street, don't look at it: cross over to the other side and continue walking in the opposite direction. Ask too much of a brand and be prepared for it to lose its soul. A brand won't be pressured; it finds its own limits, and it shows you who it is. A brand dances along the fine lines between who it claims to be, who you think it is and who history tells you it has been. Recently I have been thinking of brands as exercises *in extreme, perhaps excessive, self-consciousness*. It's time for brands to raise their awareness and get even quieter.

2014

"Hic sunt leones." – lit. "Here there are only lions." Notations on Roman maps showing the limits of empire. No point in going any further.

"No regerts." -Tattoo being removed from woman's hip, Las Vegas

"Financial Crime and Compliance Made Simple" – seminar title of 3-day MBA session in London in December 2014

Forgive my tardiness: I couldn't breathe. Let us hope that the inflection point on financial markets, the biosphere, Moore's Law and Twerking has been reached. That net neutrality has been grossly understated. That the pandemic does not fall victim to predictive modeling. That I don't lose my mind to contextual computing. That IRM and the Internet of Objections doesn't lead to an excess of secular stagnation.

update on last year's hot topics

"Being in politics is like being a football coach. You have to be smart enough to understand the game, and dumb enough to think it's important."
- Eugene McCarthy

Upstarts

If numbers alone constitute the measure of brand success, **China** beats everyone. The emerging middle class uses 600m smart phones to do every darn thing, buy plane tickets, pay bills, talk with clients, digest marketing. The world stared wide-eyed at the $25bn Alibaba IPO. A 'Lyric Coke' online campaign coordinated to messages on bottles got 3 billion views, in an environment where companies spend more on digital advertising than television. Pundits claim China moves upmarket, even in an environment where FB, YouTube,

Twitter and Gmail –favored American shopping portals- are all officially blocked. Tidy Laundry earned a hefty fine from the police after they ran a digital campaign where women stripped to their underwear on the Shanghai metro. The new monied class, set to become the largest market for space tourism, plans microgravity weddings at $100k per ticket with *taikonauts* clad in interplanetary gowns created by a couture sector hamstrung only by klutzy earthbound supply chains and low R&D priorities. Yet the government's anti-extravagance campaign soured the ultra-premium beverage category, once the favoured province of your friendly neighbourhood bureaucrat. Diageo's deployment of David Beckham to tout their sweeter downmarket whiskey targets private dinners and large family occasions rather than the lavish state banquets of yore. Unilever and Nestlé report a slowdown at the checkout counter for products like packaged food, drink, household goods, Dove Soap and Ben & Jerry's ice cream. Margarine and spreads turn out to be a drag on growth. Those Yuan-denominated bonds Sri Lanka was about to sell- swept under the carpet after a swift change of government in the strategic port of Colombo; Beijing had spent lavishly, hoping for a stronghold. The environment, let's not go there. What may turn out to be the next imperialist transgressor: refrigeration. China is about to surpass the USA in refrigerated storage capacity, a scenario rapt with environmental consequence owing to the supergreenhouse gases emitted, thousands of times more warming than CO_2.

It could be time to put your money on **India** as the next global powerhouse. A booming democracy whose internet content is driven by ABCD (astrology, Bollywood, cricket and divinity) can't be all bad. A rapidly growing under-25 age group is about to seize the reins, shedding generations of conservatism, cutting back on corruption, perhaps already the most populous nation on earth, with 400m technocrats and the 3rd largest and fastest-growing smartphone market in the world.

Brazil managed to samba through the World Cup, largely ignoring the worst drought in 80 years, and the increase in deforestation under the recent President Roussel. São Paulo, South America's biggest and wealthiest urban center, may run out of water as key reservoirs have dried up, a result of stripping 80% of natural forests along the Serra da Cantareira watersheds, which formerly fed the six artificial reservoirs sustaining the city. There's always *caipirinhas*.

and the moribund

Despite disappointing Black Friday sales, down 11% from the prior year, the Dollar strengthened after Obama appeared on the Colbert television show. An ironic landscape where the digital divide prevails, the more shocking inequality in **America** is that web access is most present in prosperous communities and strongly correlated to race and income. The US ranks 30th in the top 33 nations for affordability of internet. Unlike other economies, television still dominates marketing-world.

"I have done little justice to the Great City of Paris." - Eugene Atget

Place branding alerts

Bulgaria's booming, but not in the way you want it to. A spate of blasts at plants decommissioning land mines near Gorni Lom, and a huge explosion at the privately-owned Midzhur plant dismantling Greek munitions left the country shell-shocked. Similar episodes have multiplied in recent years in family-held ammunition facilities that pay their workers on average 240 levs ($154) per month. Most of the branded armaments date from the Communist era.

A former Joint Secretary of the Tourism Ministry wants to turn Kala Ghoda, an historic district of **Mumbai** into a 'cultural hub,' citing NYC's Times Square as his model. Despite the fact that the area seems to be regenerating on its own, the politico would like to ignore stringent building codes and place large video display screens, a huge Indian flag and costumed film and cartoon characters among the maze of century-old buildings to "communicate ambition."

No secrets

JPMorgan reported exposure of 76 million households and 8 million small businesses in a data breach, "but only one million were compromised." A year earlier about a half million prepaid cash card users suffered what the bank referred to as a smaller intrusion. The bank spent $250m in 2014 to prevent such incidents. In June, **Spotify** asked 40 million users to re-enter log-in credentials, and urged all Android app users to upgrade in the next few days. In the same month, **EBay** told all users to change their passwords, since hackers had accessed everyone's home addresses. A hacker group called 4chan claimed they got 200,000 images from the ephemeral app **Snapchat**, who retorted that only 40,000 were taken. 4chan apologized by posting, "We're very sorry… we haven't profited from this," then announced they had discovered porn they eventually traced to Sweden and Norway, which in an episode of *digilantism* they promptly reported to child protective services. The *NYTimes* queried the hackers, who responded that in exchange for an interview they wished to be paid in **Bitcoins**, the non-traceable blackmailer's cryptocurrency of choice. **Target's** CEO resigned after a data breach which cost the retail brand $100m in related expenses compromising quarterly earnings. Venture capitalists in Silicon Valley identified **privacy protection start-ups** as a growth category for potential funding. The next frontier of digital bounty: **voiceprints**. Corporate and government databases begin to build vast libraries of utterances which can be used to pay pensions, collect taxes or track criminals, more reliable than fingerprints. As always, the downside will be the potential for surveillance.

"You can hide almost anything except the atmosphere."
– Jean-Pierre Baratin

Small wonder they call it the web

IBM divested itself of its chip division, paying Globalfoundries Inc. $1.5bn and throwing in access to its IP to take the unprofitable business unit off its hands. **Intel** passed the landmark of 100m chips shipped, looking ahead to the burgeoning wearables category; emerging markets like China and Latin America are proving weaker than established markets like the USA. **Instagram** passed 200m users, and offered easier, more sophisticated tools of curation, stoking the fires of jealousy among aficionados.

A paper from the National Academy of Sciences revealed that **Facebook** tweaked the newsfeeds of 700,000 users, in a study designed to investigate claims that emotions could be influenced by manipulating language. In a program of undetectable maneuvering, select negative stories went out to unwitting readers. The company then analyzed correspondence, surveying word choice to determine whether people were bummed out. No discussion of the ethics, or a hint that it might have been unacceptable experimenting on people over social media without their consent.

Marketers appear to have lost their appetite for **cookies**. Users now access the internet from a myriad of devices. Sophisticated blocking tools mean half of all machines can no longer be cookied. Behavior, leads and conversions now require more critical surveying across multiple devices, to identify particular individuals and browsers, patterns, or likely users.

The increasing popularity of instant messages (50bn IMs sent every day) heralds the slow demise of **SMS**. But marketers continue to love SMS, a medium which refuses to be ignored. 98% of SMS get opened, developing countries have fewer smartphones, and texts turn out to be an effective way to interact with customers.

A **fake Android app**, tracked back to Mainland China, circulated during the Occupy Central pro-democracy movement in Hong Kong. Those who opened the app secretly unpacked malware which allowed the Death Star to read and receive messages, record phone calls and geolocate. Thousands downloaded it before it was unmasked.

Netflix accounts for more than 35% of non-mobile bandwidth usage in US/Canada during peak hours; the rest gets eaten by gamers. Netflix streaming service boasts 50 million global subscribers. The growth of cable and satellite subscriptions has stalled, since you get a lot of stuff you don't want, and the internet allows more selectivity. Sony, DirecTV and Showtime now launching internet products. Sports are the one major component holding the cable bundle together.

Watch out, TV. We have seen the future and its name is **YouTube**. Every minute 100 hours of video and 300 hours of new content are uploaded; every day one billion people worldwide watch more than 300m hours of video; 83% of internet users in the US watch video on the site. Cable TV will be gone in a decade, and why not? YouTube, a global platform seen in 200 countries, offers more instantaneous data than TV. Today's media stars, *vloggers*, have evolved into floggers for product and corporate endorsements. They cost less, and appear to deliver seemingly honest and personal recommendations direct to target. Companies like Pepsi advertise more on digital platforms than on conventional media.

Bye-bye, **Freemium**. Angry Birds, once the most popular casual gaming app, has changed its business since disillusion has set in over upgrades costing as much as $60. In the face of falling net profits, a 50% plunge in one year, Rovio's CEO was kicked out of the nest. The company now generates half its income from licensing: movies, animation, product, theme parks. Companies like King and Rovio valued in billions at IPO see declining interest. The only legacy Candy Crush may leave is a big cavity.

Technophile, commitment-phobic millennials unable to forge relationships IRL ("in real life") now meet, rendezvous and break up online. **Tinder**, a popular virtual dating app, allows perfunctory swiping left or right on the small screen to curate friendships. The New Velocity helps users to pump up their neurological responses in hyper-real time, altering hormonal states and promoting the release of dopamine without an old-fashioned physical hook-up. Young college men are less inclined to seek out a three-dimensional partner, and fill in the gaps with online porn.

"This is worse than being in love with a grasshopper." – Gun moll to gangster boyfriend in original version of *Scarface* **(1932)**

All a big game

In the late 1990s, the **South Korean** government focused on internet and telecommunications infrastructure development. Today the country is video game-crazy. Competitive gaming now forms a part of mainstream culture, with parlors called *PC bangs* equivalent to the neighbourhood basketball courts found in the West. Teens go to meet up with friends, and visits to such clubs are as common as dates for the movies. Huge tournaments now the norm, with 40K fans filling a stadium to watch top gamers compete. There's official concern about the cut-throat monomaniacal focus which has led to epidemic game-addiction. Reports of gamers dying of exhaustion, after days of uninterrupted play. The South Korea National Assembly advises, "The best way to avoid addiction is for families to play games together."

In the USA, a feminist cultural critic, Anita Sarkeesian, challenged how **women** are portrayed in video games. She was forced to cancel a talk at Utah State University after she became the target of harassment by enraged gamers who threatened violence. USU received email that a massacre would be carried out against attendees of the event. School police told Sarkeesian that under Utah law they could not prevent attendees from bringing concealed weapons to the speech.

The big game hunt is on for the vanishing species called **sports franchises**. The value of teams soars as cable companies battle to hold onto consumers' attention with premium content. A little known feature of the US tax code allows buyers to claim half of the purchase price of a team as a deduction over fifteen years, which may explain Steve Ballmer's recent grab of the LA Clippers. It translates into a $1bn writeoff.

"We try to explicitly view ourselves as not editors." – Greg Marra, head engineer of team that designs FB NewsFeed algorithms

Information ecology

Keyword search sounds simplistic, but **social eclipsing search** could be the attractive new traffic driver for marketers. The algorithm considers word combinations and groupings to array search results, ignoring pages optimized for specific terms.

The incidence of **online incivility** rises. The phenomenon called trolling often follows episodes of impulse-control problems, exacerbated by the New Velocity. Compounding this, now that the internet has become central to the human experience, the distance between celebrities and critics has compressed. An embittered wire-head is suspected of being the hacker who exposed Sony's private emails to public scrutiny.

Kim Kardashian sits near the level of Albert Einstein, with her fluency across multiple platforms including TV and social media. She licensed her media-self as the main character of a video game which earned $1.6bn in revenue in its first five days on the market, the fifth highest grossing game in Apple's app store. Lending more than her likeness and voice, she cross-promoted it on her Instagram and Twitter accounts, augmenting her posts with intermittent views of her nether region. The game is free for users to download, but offers a multitude of opportunities to make *in-app purchases*. No wonder she and Kanye could afford a $20m wedding. Another reminder of the price paid for celebrity: the surrender of your privacy, the end of mystery.

Millennials consume the better part of their news digitally, largely through social media. **Facebook** has 1.3bn users, logging on monthly, and drives 20% of all traffic to news sites. FB's News Feed, the prime driver, is directed by a 26-year old engineer, who can choreograph the rise or fall of a news site depending on how it performs. Fragmentation is the new reality: publishers increasingly reach readers through single articles rather than complete editions. Content is created for *the way it is being consumed*. Other factors influencing the svengalis: how a user came to the article, which device they are on, and -if on a mobile phone- which way they are holding it, time of day, location.

Google News figures less in publisher's growth strategies, supplanted by FB, whose news traffic dominates. Axel Springer, Germany's biggest news publisher, imposed a 2-week blackout on Google's access to its content, and discovered a 40% drop in traffic from the info behemoth. Google likes you if you write in their particular heuristic-friendly voice: the language regular people use, the most important keywords at the beginning of a headline.

Continuing reports on the battering of **pulp news**. Heavy investment in trucks and presses has disappeared, and newsrooms downsize. Delivery of the *Orange County Register* print edition halted after the paper failed to pay the *LA Times* for the service. Reporters and employees were asked to field phone calls from irate subscribers. Incentivized staffers who handled 20 calls over 2 days became eligible to win four Maine lobsters, fresh steamers and New England Clam Chowder. Reporters asked to deliver copies were advised to bring along a companion to help toss papers and navigate the route.

Audiobooks, long regarded as the forgotten spinster of the publishing industry, reincarnate under a new name, **audio entertainment**. New titles won't be based on print at all, conceived and produced as digital fodder, along the same lines as what happened to HBO and Netflix when they transformed into content creators. New titles in the product-hungry sector will resemble old-time radio dramas, integrating music and sound effects, and never see an analog page.

Proficiency on the keyboard may be a fast and efficient alternative to **handwriting**, but at the expense of greater neural activation in areas of the brain associated with working memory. Freehand scribing of letterforms evidences increased activity in the *left fusiform gyrus*, the *inferior frontal gyrus* and the *posterior parietal cortex*. In a study conducted, children who typed or traced the letter or shape showed no such effect. Indications are that only the actual effort which engages the brain's motor pathways delivers the learning benefits of handwriting, said to extend beyond childhood.

Baby talk, aka *Parentese*, the cloying simpering squeaky voice commonly imposed on innocent tots, turns out to be of little value, even when dispensed in quantity. Scientists at Temple University found quality interactions using rich terminology infinitely more valuable than goo-goo ga-ga. The total number of words has no correlation to future ability. Shared symbols, understanding of ritual and conversational fluency result from holding to a higher standard of erudition.

Putting down mobile devices

North Korea's first public mobile network was launched in 2008, and now over 2 million subscribe, mostly members of the elite class. A quarterly culture magazine published a list of phone etiquette guidelines for users. "Speaking loudly or arguing over the phone in public places... is thoughtless and impolite behaviour." The article advises that people should introduce themselves when accepting a call to avoid inquiries such as, "Hello? Is it you, comrade Yeong-cheoi?"

Apple, the most valuable company in the world at $747bn, sold 10m iPhone6 and 6 Plus phones in the first 3 days on sale. This after 39 million units flew off the shelves the prior quarter. In the US, iPhones make up about 40% of smartphones in use, though Android phones are more popular elsewhere. Apple's mobiles account for a disproportionately large percentage of the company's profits, 60-70%, and for 18% of the entire rise and 3-5% of the weighting of the S&P index for 2014. It is estimated that iPhone sales add one-quarter to one-third of a percentage point to the annualized growth rate of the GNP. *The Economist* ought to discontinue the Big Mac Index and launch an iPhone iNdex. The iWatch made its debut to design raves, under a fashion accessory disguise - Apple dumped wellness/medical applications, confounded by privacy and software issues, but still ordered a hefty 5m initial production run in hopes that brand loyalty will drive sales. ApplePay had problems which could only be resolved by replacing the phone. Ouch! Weird speculations and ulterior motives hinted that Apple might buy Tesla in 18 months, but Musk denied it. China has 50 million iPhones in use, though the grey market for smuggled devices dried up. The government clamped down on illegal traffic, intercepting speedboats, seizing phones stashed in secret compartments and axles of trucks. Shanghai bureaucrats were instructed to use PRC-manufactured Huawei phones, and office workers in Beijing no longer bring Apple computers or tablets to work, since they represent a conspicuous display of wealth.

The Last Days of Advertising

Scientists survey raw brain data to unlock the mysteries of consumer choice. They aim to determine why we prefer some products and brands over others, using the tools of **neuromarketing**, monitoring signals located in the *nucleus accumbens*, tracking the intensity of visceral responses such as anger, lust, disgust and excitement. It all comes down to significant changes in the blood flow in that part of the brain, capitalizing on the marketing value of subconscious cerebral data. Almost time to bring in the product designers.

Eye contact provides a cognitive jump start that humans crave. Those who avoid it are more likely to suffer from depression and feelings of isolation. Breaking it to consult the small screen degrades your social facility and emotional intelligence. Eye contact's magnetic and mesmeric effect plays an essential role in developing emotional stability and social fluency, and makes us more aware and empathetic. It's suspected *emoticons* may fulfil some of this unconscious need. Researchers at Cornell University manipulated the rabbit's eyes on a Trix cereal box and found that adult subjects were more likely to choose it over competing brands on the same shelf. Rembrandt had an intuitive inkling of this; his portrait subjects' eyes follow you around the room.

The 2014 **Cannes Golden Lions** purported to champion virtual humanity, but it was more a case of the leopard not changing its spots. One *digilante*-style ad posited a web site naming hurricanes after climate-change deniers, while a second imagined a digital child avatar designed to entrap sex offenders online; a favourite internet phone service told the weepy story of a sentimental friendship in documentary style, hankies optional; a particularly irksome message depicted people at an old-age home co-opted to chat with overseas kids, essentially training the next generation of telemarketers and call center drones; and a famous skin cream touted its extra special offer of an electronic bracelet that allowed digital tracking of your kids on the sinister Brazilian beach to counter the risk of child trafficking.

Five pharmaceutical companies were named in lawsuits in Illinois and California for the **aggressive marketing of painkillers**. An epidemic of opioid addiction has led to a serious increase in related ER visits in those states. Under the pretense of funding patient information groups, the companies paid an organization called American Pain Foundation $10m to play down the addiction potential of specific drugs.

"War is discovery." - General Martin Dempsey, Chairman of Joint Chiefs of Staff, on campaign to defeat ISIS

The full-color English language magazine **Inspire** is funded by the proceeds from kidnappings, oil piracy, bank robbery and extortion. Editorial content aims at Muslims in the West: how-to articles about bomb-making; photos of Charlie Hebdo editors and cartoonists; informative statistical tables on cities taken over, decapitations [sic] committed by ISIS forces, checkpoints set up, apostates repented. Says Publisher Abu Bara al-Hindi, "The cure for depression is jihad."

Once the province of a small global network of private sellers, **Papal Blessings** will now be offered online by The Vatican. High-end parchment documents are hand-lettered, but most are computer-generated. Cost €13-25 each in various sizes, styles and colours. Sales up 50% from last year due to the new Pope's popularity.

"The cinema is an invention with no future." – Antoine Lumière, father of Louis and Auguste

"It's a whorehouse and people go mad." – Actor John Cusack on Hollywood

"Deserve's got nothing to do with it." – Clint Eastwood

Celebrity

Live for now or live forever? Dead celebrities earn substantially more than living ones. Consider the estate of Michael Jackson, who earned $140m in 2014, eight years after his demise. In the same year Elvis brought in $55m, and his heirs later sold rights to license his name to **Authentic Brands Group** for $125m. Authentic also owns rights to Marilyn Monroe. Resurrection planned for many of the dear departed in the form of holographic Vegas extravaganzas.

As of November, **Lady Gaga** had 42.7m Twitter followers. **Barack Obama** has less than 25m.

An orange and red rainbow signifying the renewal and energy of a sunrise visually identified **Oprah Winfrey**'s "The Life You Want Weekend" in Newark, Houston, Miami and Seattle. Basic registration for branded attachment to the broadcast magnate -also regarded as a spiritual guru- started at $99. Pantene-sponsored head massage, Toyota-sponsored tent, Reinvention Tent, free yoga sessions, cooking demonstrations, fashion show, free travel size tube of Crest and a small bag of Tide capsules, $15 pre-ordered Oprah box lunch (half a sandwich, apple, bag of chips, water), and the opportunity to join Oprah's Circle of Friends ($199, included tiered magazine subscription + fan club + birthday card personally sent by Oprah). Add-ons at branded boutique: book $25; soul library $79; t-shirt $38; hoodie $60; phone cover $20. Attendees say they go in search of what they have been missing. Oprah transparent on stage at conclusion, "Thank you for your money."

Maria Vanessa Perez promises that one day she will be President of the USA. To encourage her, former sports team owner Donald Sterling gave her a $1.8m residence, a Ferrari, 2 Bentleys, a Range Rover and a security detail. Under the new persona **V. Stiviano** she appeared for a throng of reporters, speaking from behind a Daft Punk mask at LA's Farmer's Market and refused to give an interview.

Grey economics

A concerned citizen asks, "Why are there so few apps designed for **old people**?" Ironically, the senior sector represents the numerical majority, with the highest spending power. Yet the aging population is a drag on growth. Old eyes can't easily read small text; old hands can't manipulate the buttons; old people don't engage in casual gaming. A conspiracy suspected to exclude grey hairs from successfully operating mobile devices.

Luxury

Let's be honest, what with the warm embrace of internet-borne marketing, it's high time to split the luxury category into two distinct identifiable sectors. **Fast Moving Luxury Goods** (call them FMLGs) have adopted the techniques and platforms of mass production and consumer products, with their only distinction being brand association and price points. **Slow Moving Luxury Goods** (SMLGs) retain the quality of true uniqueness, hand crafting, high cost and you have to wait for them. The greatest differentiator: patience.

Arnault accepted a conciliation procedure after paying an €8m penalty for stealthy acquisition of fugitive **Hermès** shares. He had gathered a quarter of group's ownership by trawling disgruntled heirs and via shadow company transactions. Agreed not to buy any more shares for 5 years.

A used 2013 Hermès Birkin handbag, in dyed brown and beige croc was offered by **Heritage**, a NYC auction house, for $115,000. The luxury accessories category is a recent addition to the auction business, and sales of handbags rank second behind timepieces. **Christie's** succumbs to the New Velocity with a Buy-It-Now feature online, designed to capture younger customers under the age of 45, half who register to bid - average price of items offered on their site $11K. A yellow gold 2000 Patek Philippe watch went for $195K after the seller posted an Instagram photo.

Space Tourism took a nosedive when **Virgin**'s Spaceship Two *augured in* due to pilot error. Nobody cancelled their reservation and Branson vowed to forge ahead on delivery of the third spacecraft. A privately funded venture called **Aeroscraft** wants to launch a 770 foot long dirigible for long-haul freight. 250 ton capacity, 5870 mile range. Airships suffer a perception problem, no thanks to Led Zeppelin, though non-flammable helium fills today's leviathan gasbags.

Looking to appeal to the premium buyer, **Starbucks** launched The Reserve to meet the growing market for high-end coffees, some which sell for as much as $45 a pound. Products don't carry the ubiquitous mermaid signature, only a star with an "R". An estate in Costa Rica was purchased to produce specialty beans exclusively for the company.

Science class

Aromatherapy the key to immortality? Researchers at the University of Chicago found that people with the poorest **sense of smell** were at the greatest risk for early demise. The bottom 39%, the least sensitive noses, sniffed no longer, 4 years after being tested. Scientists believe the sense of smell is intimately linked to health and wellbeing, but exactly how it correlates remains unclear. Olfactory brand gurus snorted at the news.

Official delivery of **nicotine** in transformation: call it *tabac noir*. Swedish **snus**, little pouches of shredded evil leaf you lodge between gum and inside cheek, present a significantly smaller risk of oral cancer. The anti-breath freshener does present an increase in the risk of pancreatic cancer and users expel a gruesome brown juice, besmirching the environment. **Vaping**, electronic delivery of tobacco distillate through largely unregulated fashion accessories experiences incendiary growth, kind of like smoking air freshener. Big cigarette brands have bought up competitors, but many concoctions manufactured in China considered suspiciously risky still sold on the high street. Vapers are also a favorite way to smoke the other kind of weed. Australia banned overt branding on **ciggie packaging**, and found that sales immediately dropped. Obama, a compulsive Nicorette gum-chewer, reopened diplomatic relations with Cuba, lighting up the hearts of American **Montecruz, Partagas** and **Cohiba** lovers, felons no more.

"The first billionaire in hip hop from the motherfucking West Coast," - Dr. Dre, whose real name is Andre Young, in video about Apple purchase of Beats

Trends

Speed kills, they used to quip. Increasing accelerations every day driven by thought viruses - witness the price of crude, the value of the Swiss franc, the € and the $ playing musical chairs; the surging rate of climate change, knee-bopping while waiting for the real-time web; click-here-to-buy-now; and the impatience with Moore's Law. I call it **The New Velocity.**

"The greatest asset in the world is unavailability," – Graydon Carter

Your personal privacy at risk every interaction, concealed under the barrage of high-tech noises audible 24/7. Time, silence and isolation – the ability to exercise free will over them – are all at a premium. The greatest social differentiator is the **headset**. The thicker the insulation the greater the privilege, the bigger the headset the more important the wearer. The semiotic differentiator: my capacity to screen out extraneous impulses.

The fallout may be coming in a decline of gadget-obsession. Ad-blocking is at an all-time high, people detest adverts on apps, and weekly visits to social networks in the US, China, Japan and the UK have dropped by half. British doctors voice concern over the number of people being treated for tech addiction. More than half of gadget owners internationally admit to suffering anxiety when they can't use their mobile devices. An oversubscribed Kickstarter campaign successfully funded **NoPhone**, a fake handset which simulated the exact size, weight and dimensions of a mobile phone. Advertised as totally wireless, battery-free, doesn't require software updates, shatterproof and waterproof.

The end of the production line collided with Detroit. It took only 44 hours to produce the world's first 3D printed car. **The**

Strati, made of carbon fibre reinforced plastic (ABS), costs a navigable $18K-34K, engine optional.

The *Journal of the American Medical Association* performed a very small survey just before Google sent the **Google Glass** into exile. Three subjects helped determine that the device created a clinically meaningful visual field obstruction in the upper right quadrant.

The public is still the harshest critic. The Town Council of Clacton-on-Sea, UK, removed a graffiti mural by **Banksy**. Residents complained that anti-immigration banners carried by the painted pigeons were racist. The Council apologized, claiming they did not understand it was valuable art.

Had enough of trendy fitness centers filled with impossible infernal devices, exhibitionists and people looking to hook up? **Unplug**, a salon for meditation in LA (where else?) looks like a yoga or Pilates studio, but features Buddhist coaches to help you with inner workouts. Clean, modern, secular, effortless to attend, with a gift shop. $20 per session, enlightenment included. Alternately, the over-50 crowd can hustle off to **Welcyon**, a new health club franchise for seniors. Easier machines, fewer mirrors and music programmed from the good old days.

"Environmentalism is an upper-middle-class, white movement aimed at absolution and preserving a lifestyle with a Volvo." – Charles Bowden

Two incidents of airborne volatility made the skies even less friendly to the already beleaguered traveler. In September a passenger in the United Economy Plus section used **Knee Defender**, a product which prevents the seat in the row ahead to recline. The incensed victim threw water in the user's face, the flight was diverted, both passengers removed, 2 hour delay for the everyone else. In an episode which sounds more like a **Rage Nut**, Korean Air SVP Heather Cho performed an act of Brand Destruction when she delayed an Inchon-bound flight because of the way she was served macadamia nuts, forcing a senior flight attendant to kneel in front of her and apologize. If only it had been **Nutella** incorrectly served then some of the attention might have been diverted to the world's favorite nutty chocolate spread: Nutella uses up a quarter of the world's filbert supply (also known as hazel nuts), but its other key ingredient, palm oil, is a health hazard, the production of which correlates to the destruction of the rain forests of Indonesia.

Narcissism

"With the American accent, I've had far more success with women." – Stephen Hawking, explaining one of the advantages of his new speech synthesizer.

"10 Selfies Taken Moments Before Death" – morbid posts from various websites

On September 18, the cabin of JetBlue flight 1416 filled with smoke. A guy took a smiling **Selfie**, posted it online and it went viral with over 1 million views. The flight touched down safely. It's all fair game for content, rock concerts, presidential inaugurations, elementary school plays rich with *parentrazzi*, midair near-disasters. Birth of new genres: Selfies of My Divorce, Selfies at Funerals.

A **terminology survey** at San Diego State University studied 760,000 books published between 1960 and 2008. The use of "we" and "us" declined by 10%; instances of "I" and "me" increased by 42%.

Id-IOT-ic?

Apple's wristband, Nike's new generation of sensory footwear, Google's Glass, Microsoft's 3D specs mean we have crossed over the threshold into the era of **programmable objects** which sense, capture and exchange information. Developers say the most interesting contextual computing is happening with phones, so beware. Debate rages about who owns the information, whether the mysterious "they" have our best interests at heart. Fifteen years ago a panelist at the IHT Luxury Summit predicted a world where your sweater would be your best friend. Things which mimic the mythological tools of folklore and fantasy, like Excalibur, Snow White's mirror, or Woody Allen's Orgasmitron from *Sleeper* will populate the 26bn sensors forecast to be installed by 2020. As long as they don't pressure me to upgrade to the paid version, or track my YouTube visits I guess I am OK with the phenomenon. But when the sensors try to respond to my feelings by monitoring my facial expressions, the moment when algorithms decide to alter my emotions, uh-oh. A company called Affdex readies a suite of products which assess emotional connection with advertising, brands and media. When information about a package is as important as me, or the thing itself, perhaps it is time for the *thing* to rethink. Did you hear the one about The Jealous Toaster, which becomes agitated when it's not used enough? Its lever waggles anxiously. It may tell the Talking Trash Can to dispose of the muesli I wanted that morning, an unconscionable act of serial killing.

"When opponent likes fast game, Hashim plays slow; when opponent likes slow, Hashim plays fast. Against big man, Hashim makes him stoop to floor with low shots. Against tennis player used to open court, Hashim hits ball all the time very close to wall. Against player wearing glasses, Hashim gives many high shots, which he has difficulty seeing because of light overhead. When Hashim teaches, he emphasizes thinking."
- Hashim Khan (1913-2014), on squash strategy

Ci vediamo

Hasta la vista to **The Duchess of Alba**, holder of over 40 titles, scion of a venerable Spanish house, whose marriage after WWII was reputed to be the most expensive in the world. Her second marriage to her confessor, a defrocked Jesuit priest 11 years her junior, was followed by her third marriage to a civil servant 25 years younger, no doubt blinded by love and her multiple cosmetic surgeries, flowery dresses, hippy hatwear, huge estates, art collection and palaces, not to mention her $4.4bn fortune. Actuarially speaking, Nobel Laureate economist **Gary Becker** totaled. His research on marriage, crime, addiction, racial discrimination and birthrates regarded all elements of society as rational economic agents. He viewed households as small factories that produce nonmarketable basics like leisure and sleeping; quantified what people are willing to pay to avoid one another's company; and rejected the assumption that individuals were motivated by the prospect of selfish material gain. Nancy Reagan's in-house astrologer **Joan Quigley** headed for the stars. On her private line thrice-daily to the First Lady to earn her monthly retainer of $3000, she helped rule the Free World, drew horoscopes to insure the favorable alignment of planets for arms control treaties, profiled Gorbachev, and moved the time of day for the Presidential inauguration by 9 minutes. Virtually every major decision was cleared in advance with her. Ronnie's favorite question reputed to be: "What does Joan say?" **Alexander Shulgin** headed off on the ultimate trip. Following a 1960 experience with mescaline this dude went forth to create or patent almost 200 mind-altering chemicals, including Ecstasy and MDMA, stimulants, depressants, aphrodisiacs, 'empathogens,' convulsants, drugs that alter hearing, drugs that slow one's sense of time, drugs that speed it up, drugs that trigger violent outbursts, drugs that deaden emotion.

"Be regular and orderly in your life like a bourgeois, so that you may be violent and original in your work." – Flaubert

the following touchpoints to debate and discussion for the coming year

Feasts of the epiphany

In 2012, **007** switched over to Heineken, shaken down by a $45m payoff. Now Special Agent Bond has gone back on the hard stuff, in a stirring partnership with Belvedere Vodka for upcoming 'Spectre' film.

Originally packaged before the 1929 market crash under the name "Bib-Label Lithiated Lemon-Lime Soda", a beloved American soft drink kept its own dirty little secret until 1948, when the critical ingredient was banned by the FDA. These days Lithium is used to treat bipolar disorder and depression. A psychiatrist recommends adding low doses of the substance to drinking water in hopes of lowering rates of suicide, murder and rape. With drug prices so inflated, wouldn't it be cheaper to bring back the old formula and simply buy everybody a bottle of classic **7-Up**?

IP continued to confound regulators. The US Supreme Court ruled against **Aereo**, a startup which provided a dime-sized antenna allowing users to grab, stream and record from major broadcasters signals, challenging the economics of the tv business. At issue: retransmission fees. Refunds issued to a half million subscribers. Said the Justices: "The spectrum that the broadcasters use...belongs to the American public."

The largest conglomerate in the USA (value: $350bn) now rebadges its family of utility companies as **Berkshire Hathaway Energy**. Also slated to rebrand its car dealership group under the same moniker, as well as licensing its name to real estate companies in Europe and Asia. Other opportunities in its portfolio: railways, insurance, manufacturing, retailing, but no plans for re-entry into textile sector, from which they took their name.

Advocates claim cannabis extends longevity. **Bob Marley**, who died in 1981, lives on as the fifth highest-earning dead celebrity in the 2013 Forbes List, scoring $20m. A Seattle-based private equity firm raised $22m in its first round financing, aimed at funding a global ganja enterprise. They hope to add another $50m to the pot in 2015. The estate already licenses its name to headphones, audio accessories and coffee. Soon to follow under the Marley Natural name: heirloom Jamaican cannabis strains, marijuana-infused skin creams and lip balms, and paraphernalia such as vaporizers and pipes based on those preferred by Bob.

Intimations of the Bolivian Marching Powder from the aptly-named Droga5, a NYC ad agency who created the "You're On" campaign for **Diet Coke** in the face of mounting competition from energy drinks like Red Bull. The uplift touted, aimed at aspiring millennials, earned skeptical sniffs from the marketplace, leading an editor at *Beverage Digest* to toot it was critical to market these beverages as delicious, refreshing and tasting good and worry less about brand image.

"Old men ought to be explorers." –T.S. Eliot

Hollywood, clueless over the ironies of a brand name, suffered box-office disappointment and a half million pirated downloads with **Expendables 3**, a geriatric action sequel starring Stallone, Gibson and Schwarzenegger. The franchise refuses to die, and now plans a female-focused spinoff called The Expendabelles.

Greenpeace co-opted the 1500-year old Nazca geoglyphs in Peru, intending to raise awareness of global warming during the UN climate talks in Lima. Instead, the publicity stunt raised awareness of trespassing, while irreparably defiling a World Heritage site and eloquently demonstrating the concept of brand arrogance.

Dreamworks dogmatic about **Lassie**, part of a $155m character library acquisition. The studio plans extensive merchandising, but no tv series or movies for the valiant pet first seen in a 1938 movie, later criticized for saccharine plots centered on childhood trauma and neuroses. Research shows the loyal, heroic and heartwarming canine has an 83% brand awareness rating. Look for product lines targeted mainly at adults. "Lassie, get Gramps!"

You wouldn't know there were continuing woes in the global toy market by looking at **Lego**. In September 2014 the family-held Danish company took the lead as world's biggest toymaker by revenue, $2bn+, surpassing Mattel, whose sales of Barbie, Hot Wheels and Fisher-Price declined. Analysts had earlier concerns over strategic fumbles in sub-lines, but the brand was saved by the fan community, who influenced extensions into multimedia. This led to a hit movie, animated content, online games, a smartphone app, film tie-ins with Harry Potter and Star Wars, partnership with the Cartoon Network, double-digit growth in all three regions of the world. Despite huge potential in Asia, an IP risk looms, especially in competitive lines. But for the moment Lego seems to have the secret formula that transforms petrochemical compounds costing $1/kg into product that sells for 75 times that figure.

Brand gymnastics for the **Mason Jar**, a 150-year old American institution. During frontier days the jars represented home preserving and canning, the metaphor for survival.

During the Depression nearly every home used them. But refrigeration and mass-produced food, tv dinners and boxed mac and cheese saw the product transform into a glass container for stray pennies, or buried in the back yard filled with rolls of $100 bills. The recession of 2008 signaled a return, with sales jumping as millennials learned to personalize their food. In a move to attract younger customers, big corps proffer plastic knockoffs filled with sugary fare, the most blatant example a replica from 7-Eleven, designed to hold Slurpees.

Brilliant idea: a user interface which employed software and invention to create a new market of underused assets. Venture capitalists romanced them, leading to a successful $1.5bn IPO which valued the 2-year old startup at $40bn. Then, banned or reviled in world capitals, accused of price-fixing, declared illegal in South Korea, discovered doing surge pricing during the Sydney hostage crisis, an unscrupulous competitor cancellation conspiracy in New York City, gouging on Valentine's Day, reprehensible conduct by drivers, and finally making a pact with the diabolical Amazon for last-mile delivery. Yet no matter what the bad news, **Uber** refuses to go *unter*.

"Thank you for your good and properly obscene letter." - Norman Mailer to Truman Capote, in a letter dated 1959

Terminology and concepts entering the mainstream in 2015:

Clickbait – Content trickery crafted to seduce unwitting website visitors

Climate refugees - humans displaced by rising sea levels, erosion or bio-fatigue.

Contextual computing – the terrain where your wearables form opinions about you in consultation with your smartphone

Digilantism – Self-appointed citizens or groups on the net who undertake to enforce their own ethical agenda, without legal authority, typically out of frustration with the status quo.

Flow – shorthand for a self-induced state of mindlessness resulting in unjustifiable complacency and self-satisfaction from activity often associated with consumerism

IRM - Influencer Relationship Marketing, touted as the new snake oil for any communications plan. [sic] "...can affect purchase decision and consideration, benefit reputation, employee retention and recruitment, and diffuse crisis."

***Shuanggui* -** secretive extralegal process used on those citizens accused of political corruption in China

Sudden-wealth syndrome – an infirmity afflicting wealthy young people, symptoms of which include heightened ambition or a lack of motivation, feelings of shame, or the deleterious effects of inherited wealth. See also: *Affluenza*.

Underconsumptionist theory – an idea popularized by John Maynard Keynes that people inherently underspend once they become prosperous

Unicorns – fledgling tech startups valued at $1 billion following IPO

Vax kooks – opponents of vaccines, as referred to by big pharma-funded special interest groups

What is a brand?

A brand is a signal for trust
A brand is a tool of transformation
A brand is a potential obfuscation which if unscrupulously employed can conceal an organization's true nature.
A brand balances idealism and commercialism.
A brand is the last defense of Romanticism.

Recently I have thought about brands as *anchors of connection*.

2013

"The desk is a dangerous place from which to view the world." –John LeCarré

"Prediction is very difficult, especially about the future." - Niels Bohr

"I write to the vulgar, more than to the learned." – Jonathan Swift

"A developed country is not a place where the poor have cars. It's where the rich use public transportation." – Mayor of Bogota

Is there such a thing as a good drone? The word means different things to Pashtuns, Amazon, or the Queen Bee. Raise your hand if you've seen enough selfies. I don't want my relationship to be managed, no thank you. If the world is too grey, too slow for millennials, it may explain why teens don't want to drive; given the option they choose texting. All but one of the old paradigms coined by *People*'s founding managing editor have turned upside down: Young isn't better than old. Pretty *isn't* better than ugly. Rich *isn't* better than poor. Film stars *no longer* outsell television and music stars. Anything *doesn't* sell better than politics. Only nothing *still* sells better than a dead celebrity.

update on last year's hot topics

Upstarts

The Chinese puzzle prevails. To commemorate the 120th anniversary of his birth, a statue of **Chairman Mao** went on display in Shenzhen. The seated life-size figure is covered in gold and inlaid with gems valued at $16.5 million, a "solemn, austere and practical" commemoration as decreed by Xi Jinping. **Killer smog and heavy haze** in China's north and east closed highways and airports. The Ministry of Environmental Protection blamed weather conditions, motor vehicle exhaust and coal consumption. The US Embassy ordered air purifiers for all its offices. **Soil pollution** also a concern. One-sixth of China's arable land is tainted, affected by heavy metals, mostly cadmium from industrial runoff, toxic to the food chain. **A bridge over the Pan River** collapsed during severe flooding, days after a refurbishment was completed. Five dead and seven missing. Government officials and construction managers were sentenced to prison terms related to the incident. The severest sentence was given to an official who received a $20k bribe. **Chinese consumers** exceeded expectations on an annual Singles' Day online event, spending more than twice what shoppers in the US bought on Cyber Monday. Big brands and Western etailers like e-commerce as a way to sell in remote areas, where few of them have brick-and-mortar stores. **Apple and China Mobile** are bringing the iPhone to the Chinese carrier, the largest wireless network in the world, also the most fickle, where market share shifts quickly. China's **textile industry** is moving from low price exports to a time where productivity, product innovation and domestic demand are the new priorities. Companies know little about consumer expectations and even less about premium brand management and can't yet generate market insights, understand competition or create distinctive brand identity. The challenge: tame the complexities of design, marketing and distribution. **Daniel Boulud** closed his haute cuisine Beijing restaurant after a 5-year run, citing disputes with local partners; he's considering a new location in red hot Shanghai.

For technology startups, **India** carries much less political risk and better infrastructure than other emerging nations. Entrepreneurs confront bureaucratic hurdles in licensing and filings, and pressure for bribes. Indian tech employees are restless. Young hires often quit within three months to get a pay raise elsewhere. Oddly, there's a "lack of coolness" associated with new ventures. Indians are less eager for stock options than their counterparts in the United States. Royal Enfield, a division of Eicher, relaunched the Bullet model motorcycle, aimed at the international market, "handcrafted in Chennai."

Mr. Putin freed Khodorkovsky and Pussy Riot, signaling that **Russia** desperately needs more foreign investment to help upgrade crumbling infrastructure projects and to diversify its flagging economy. If the **Sochi Olympics** go smoothly, will offshore capitalists experience Volgograd amnesia?

Brasil expects to receive droves of foreign tourists around June for the **World Cup**. But Rio has only about 55,400 hotel beds to accommodate as many as 300,000 expected visitors. Residents of *favelas* are making the most of the city's acute shortage, renting out their homes to fans from around the globe, inflating already high room rates. Some World Cup construction projects like the new metro line won't be complete in time. The collapse of a stadium crane didn't help place branding, especially when a São Paulo newspaper reporter at the scene was beaten by guards and had pictures of the accident deleted from his cellphone by an Odebrecht engineer.

Despite the cacophony of protest and discord, the newest emerging economic zone may be **TIME** (Turkey Israel MidEast), where expediencies of trade, cooperation and prosperity trump fundamentalist rhetoric. Good luck, guys.

and the moribund

On Black Friday, **Americans** spent $1.7 billion less than in 2012, traditionally the biggest shopping day of the year. Yet the DJIA and S&P 500 indexes outperformed their peak levels before the financial crisis, signaling soft recovery. Still no universal health coverage, and an embarrassing launch for the Affordable Care Act website.

Alcohol related crime in the **UK** is estimated to cost the economy £11 billion a year. Young Brits go out to get blitzed, often with violent behavior the result. Half of all violent crime in Britain is alcohol-related. Half a million estimated to be collecting food aid. Retailers and supermarkets reported a surge in the theft of high value fresh food – including meat, cheese and fresh coffee – another indicator of the economic strife.

Japan's homeless men are willing to accept minimum wage to work on the clean-up of radioactive fallout around Fukushima. Recruiters get a bounty of $100 a head, candidates often found sleeping in subways. On another front, office workers from companies across Japan gathered for the 50th year to compete for the title of Japan's best phone answerer in the All-Japan Phone-Answering Competition. The contest, dominated by women, is judged on politeness and eloquence, but also serves as a reminder of the clerical positions Japanese women - often referred to as "office ladies" - still hold.

"The feminist agenda is not about equal rights for women. It is about a socialist, anti-family political movement that encourages women to leave their husbands, kill their children, practice witchcraft, destroy capitalism and become lesbians." -- Pat Robertson, from a 1992 fundraising letter

"I used to have so many opinions before I learned the facts." –Yair Lapid

Dogged by snoops

A regional court in Versailles is examining whether **IKEA** executives in France broke the law by ordering extensive personal surveillance of workers since 2002. In a case which brought to light dubious behavior, a female employee's personal data were provided to a private detective, because HR suspected she exaggerated medical claims. Eventually she was awarded nearly €60,000 in compensation. The company has publicly expressed regret that certain managers took actions that were "contrary to our values and ethics standards".

The gamification of trash, **Project BinCam**, under study in Britain and Germany, alleges to help determine if you are doing a good job of sorting recyclables. Data is collected by cameras located in your rubbish bin. Your score is computed and compared to those of other sorters via the Net. If you win, you will be rewarded with praise. Do a bad job and you risk becoming a social castoff.

Privacy laws are a muddle in the USA, with states and the Federal government often at odds. Tech companies fear some laws will harm their bottom lines, what the chief privacy counsel at Microsoft refers to as "burdensome compliance." Texas passed a bill that requires warrants for email searches. Oklahoma passed a law meant to protect the privacy of student data. At least three states proposed measures to regulate who inherits digital data, including FB passwords, when a user dies. Eight states passed laws this year limiting the use of drones. Florida is considering a draft bill that would prohibit schools from collecting biometric data to verify who gets free lunches and who gets off at which bus stop. Vermont has limited the use of data collected by license plate readers. California passed online privacy bills giving children the right to erase social media posts; making it a misdemeanor to publish identifiable nude pictures online without the subject's permission; and requiring companies to tell consumers whether they abide by "do not track" signals on web browsers. Stiff lobbying efforts stopped a bill in California requiring any business that retains a customer's personal information share a copy of that information at the customer's request, and disclose which third parties received the information.

You got *gibier*

Domino's makes optimum use of gamification. Visit their web site and create your own pizza; it's both a scheme for product introduction, and can be used as an ordering mechanism. You then play a game to track real-time progress of your order to delivery, and HR uses the utility as a recruitment tool. **Coca-Cola** set up interactive games between India and Pakistan, large display video terminals linking Mumbai-Karachi, where players mimic moves and gestures, finding points of commonality instead of difference.

A Bitcoin-fused

Since the Winkelvoss Twins are involved, it may be a good idea to review their history with FB. The boys are betting deep on the hot bubbling cryptocurrency **Bitcoin**, created or generated or mined -whatever- when computers solve a set of algorithms. Back in 2010 a Jacksonville, Florida software geek named Laszlo Hanyecz traded 10,000 Bitcoins, at that time worth about 0.003 cent apiece, in exchange for two Papa John's pizzas. Tab for the pies delivered: $30. "The idea of trading them for a pizza was incredibly cool," Mr. Hanyecz recalls. Within a year the same coins were worth $1,242. Today they would be worth $1.7 million. A Norwegian man who invested $22 in the virtual currency four years ago forgot about them, until he read reports of rising value, and realized his coins were now worth $850,000. He bought an upmarket flat in Oslo by selling a fifth of his stake. In 2013 an Australian man who ran an online "wallet service" for storing Bitcoins claimed hackers stole 4100 Bitcoins (valued at US$1.04m) from his site, taken in two separate attacks. He said he would not report the theft to police. Bitcoin transactions are virtually impossible to trace. Some users suspected an inside job. In a radio interview the man, who used only his online name, denied being involved. "I know this doesn't mean much, but I'm sorry, and saying that I'm very sad that this has happened is an understatement. Please don't store Bitcoins on an internet-connected device, regardless if it is your own or a service's."

Orbital maneuvers

Originally intended to destabilize Iranian nuclear reactors, **Stuxnet** rocketed onto the International Space Station via infected USB drives, a digital payload unwittingly brought aboard by Russian cosmonauts. The interstellar virus dematerialized after Microsoft was jettisoned in favor of open source Linux operating systems. A fitting metaphorical lesson for the final frontier?

"I fear the day that technology will surpass our human interaction. The world will have a generation of idiots." –Albert Einstein

Social media

The Guardian reported that YouTube replaced FB as kids' favorite site.

Zuckerberg's hot-babe-engine morphed into the preferred web destination of Mum, Dad, Gramps and Granny. Users aged 18 to 29, citing **FB fatigue**, said they expected to spend even less time on the site in the coming year, giving thumbs down to tedious and irrelevant content.

A Twitter founder is backing a long-form blogging site called Medium, yet another platform which doesn't pay and where anyone can be a writer. Didn't anybody alert him that's already the name of **Regis Debray**'s intellectual French journal about the transmission of knowledge to future generations?

Snapchat, the anti-FB, offers its users impermanence, privacy and anonymity, not to mention an easy way to send sexually suggestive photos which disappear within 10 seconds. It now processes upward of 350 million messages a day, about a six-fold increase in traffic since a year ago. Pursuing a Microsoft strategy (eat the competition), Zuckerberg offered nearly $3 billion for the startup, which founders publicly turned down. Shortly after, FB launched Poke, a similar product which never took off. Gibson Security, a group of anonymous hackers from Australia, published a report detailing an unresolved Snapchat security vulnerability which can reveal phone numbers of users, as well as their privacy settings.

Beyoncé proved how bored she is with old school music marketing moves. When it came time to release her newest album product, she ignored radio, TV appearances, retail and brand partnerships. Instead, she simply wrote, "Surprise!" to her more than eight million Instagram followers, and put the full album up for sale on iTunes, selling 365,000 copies in the US on its first day.

High school seniors take note: **college admissions officers** now routinely visit an applicant's personal social media pages to learn more about them. 30 percent of admissions officers surveyed said they had discovered information online that had negatively affected an applicant's prospects. Guidance counselors now advise kids on how to sanitize their digital identities.

I wanna hold your handheld

Motorola's new lower-priced phone won't release in China, the biggest market for low-end phones in the world. And not because users there typically switch their handheld devices every six months. Motorola thinks Moto G will appeal to people in places like **Brazil, Chile** and **Peru**, where there are more than 500 million potential customers. The device features a big high-resolution screen and runs the latest Android software and apps. The phone will also be offered in Europe, then India and Southeast Asia and the United States, where Motorola bets Moto G will appeal to people who can't get a fancy smartphone, particularly **children**.

A survey found that 38% of children **under 2** had used mobile devices like iPhones, tablets, or Kindles. On average these digital kiddies spend an hour a day in front of screens - watching television, using computers, viewing DVDs, playing with mobile apps. Kids 2 to 4 can't be marketed to, but still average two hours a day. Television dominates, taking up about half of all children's screen media time. The American Academy of Pediatrics recommends that children under 2 should have no screen time. But this hasn't prevented the appearance of an expanding category of **baby apps**.

Ebooks can't turn the page

Social Books, Rethink Books, Push Pop Press, Copia, Small Demons sound familiar to you? Didn't think so. They were epublishing start-ups who tried to harness social reading apps or multimedia and leaned on programmer capabilities rather than reader's needs. They never successfully reimagined the core experience of the book. Lamented author Peter Meyers, "We pursued distractions and called them enhancements."

How are you feeling about Big Data?

Measurement lovers say data-driven insights will soon alter the balance in how decisions are taken. Decisions of all kinds, they believe, will increasingly be formed on the basis of data and analysis rather than experience and intuition - more science and less sneaking suspicion.

"It's not true that I had nothing on. I had the radio on."
–Marilyn Monroe

Celebrity

Prior to announcing his intention to retire in December, 19-year old **Justin Bieber** ushered in the next episode of his personal reality series by visiting Centauros, the most famous bordello in Rio; he stayed 3 hours, then left under a bedsheet. **James Franco**, writing in the *NYTimes*, believes that selfies are the main issue when it comes to social networking. "I try to post a selfie with a puppy, a topless selfie or a selfie with Seth Rogen, because these are all things that are generally liked." **Stefani Germanotta** went public with her fears that "sensitive, private" information may "inflict significant personal and professional harm" upon her if laid bare in someone else's lawsuit. The transparent pop star pleaded with the court to quash information that a former BF and BFF might disclose in their own battle over who discovered whom and how much revenue siphoned from her career they must redress.

trendseekers alerts

It's Rollerball

Talent agents figured out that there's no future in the increasingly troubled businesses of movies and television. The last decade has seen plummeting DVD revenues, turning the film industry, formerly a growth business, into a flat or declining enterprise. Today's focus has shifted to the more predictable world of **sports, athletic careers and events**, where athletes command contracts worth hundreds of millions of dollars. The big money will be in negotiating endorsement, licensing and media-rights deals. William Morris' $2.3 billion offer for IMG creates a mega-agency vastly more powerful than its primary rival, puny CAA. Probably a good time to re-watch Norman Jewison's 1975 classic starring James Caan, which suddenly doesn't look so far-fetched.

"You don't understand it unless you can afford it."
—Pascal Sommariba

The luxury category

Tata's effort to gain a share of the Chinese luxury car market is good news for **Jaguar** lovers. The brand launched the 2014 F-Type, its first pure two-seat sports car in 40 years. The 495-horsepower V8 growls off the starting line at $92,895.

Neiman Marcus sold a new category of luxury experience along with a $1.85 million 25-carat rough diamond offered in their 2013 Christmas Book. The stone comes with a trip to Africa, a comprehensive tour enabling the buyer to track its provenance from source to final cut and personalized bauble design.

Echoes of **Costa Concordia** may explain why the city of Venice finally banned those preposterous cruise ships that have been defiling the Giudecca Canal.

In an unlikely brand partnership, **Gagosian** collaborated with **Leica** to create a limited edition paint-splattered X2 camera for $3000.

Burberry fearlessly harnessed the power of social media to promote its brand. The 156-year old company has successfully reinvented itself several times over, seeing its fastest growth in online sales. A huge effort in China taps into the world's most vibrant luxury market, using homegrown social media sites and celebrity endorsements. Never heard of Chen Kun? The Chinese heartthrob posted twice to his 48 million web followers from a Burberry menswear show. With virtual runway projections in retail outlets, unconventional promotions and iPads in the hands of every retail clerk, the brand seems to be successfully weathering the storm of new territory exploitation.

"Whatever you say, say nothing." – Seamus Heaney

Ciao ciao

World Citizen #1 **Garry Davis**, who issued passports, identity cards, birth and marriage certificates, postage stamps and currency, and periodically ran unopposed for President of the World, left for the big meeting in the sky. His parting administrative acts were sending passports to Assange and Snowden. **Lawrence G. Foster** checked out, credited with writing the definitive PR Rx on how to take a bitter pill, following the Tylenol cyanide crisis. Nods and waves to **Clifford Nass**, who determined that multi-taskers are terrible at ignoring irrelevant information, keeping it neatly organized, and at switching from one task to another. **Maxine Powell**, who directed Motown's in-house charm school during its glory years, shimmied offstage at 98. Supreme sacrifice and yielding not to temptations, she shaped the style of legendary soul singers before stopping in the name of love.

the following touchpoints to debate and discussion for the coming year

Dognitive fluency

A researcher at the Center for Mind/Brain Sciences of the University of Trento in Italy has determined that when a dog swings its tail to the right, it signals relaxation. A wag to the left seems to induce stress. It is believed that the wagging directions might arise from automatic responses rooted in the different hemispheres of the canine brain. The Pet Product Manufacturers Association estimates $56 billion spent on pets in the US in 2013. A new possibility for focus groups, or are we barking up the wrong tree?

Brand resurrection

Twinkies spontaneously reincarnated. Hostess Brands LLC, parent company of the favorite American junk food, saddled with a $1.3 billion pile of debt, filed for bankruptcy when they couldn't come to terms with unions. The market experienced a sugar crash. Brand loyalty and customer demand won out. Under new management and a reorganization, 50 million of the cream-filled snack cakes zoomed back to grocery shelves in record time. Also returned from the dead: beloved Hostess sub-brands **Cup Cakes, Zingers, Ho-Hos, Do-nettes, Ding-Dongs and Sno-Balls.**

Terminology and concepts entering the mainstream in 2014

Connection technologies- digital media allowing largely unrestricted sharing of photos

Dude-*oier* – to address someone in French as "Dude"

Ephemeral encryption – a system where encryption keys are generated between two users as they are communicating, and then destroyed

Hadoop – an open-source software framework being used in mood-detecting, touted as a means to exploit and monetize sentiment analysis

Hikikomori - a term used to describe the estimated 1 million Japanese young people who withdraw into their rooms

Phablet – a phone/tablet hybrid challenging conventional handsets

Regenerative medicine – Adios repair, hola grow-a-new-one

"You know when Keith disagrees. He normally pulls a knife on you."
–Ron Wood, on Keith Richards

What is a brand?

This year I question whether brands are disembodied concepts transportable between organizations. A brand is the central idea that drives an organization towards its purpose, thus it's a highly individualized entity. There is no such thing as a bad organization; only bad parents. Every interaction is an opportunity for brand value to increase. How close to the brand you are is inversely proportional to the amount of noise made by the brand. Thus quiet brands are still of interest. A brand explains an organization's existence.

Recently I have thought about brands as *abstractions* which explain an organization's existence.

2012

"The time to buy is when blood is running in the streets."
– Baron Nathan Rothschild (1777-1836)

"Don't you DARE take the name of Texas in vain." – Sponge Bob

Once brands lose sight of the customer, the game changes. Brand professionals need to remember their role as advocates. This year the dialogue centers on the experience, and how to keep customers connected. The dilemma concerns the ethic of consumption. Haven't we had enough? We are still caught up in the vicious enterprise of contentment aligned with the retail experience. Co-creation carries an implied aspect of narcissistic seduction. Have we forgotten the discussion about de-growth? The notion of consequence: old models of growth and profit ignore the pressing issues of waste and cultural egocentrism. I'm still waiting to hear scenarios of less.

update on last year's hot topics

"When facts change, I change my opinion. What do you do, sir?"
– John Maynard Keynes

Upstarts

Apple suspended iPhone4 sales in **China** after organized scalpers hired minions of rural workers to stand in line at retail stores to purchase the new device. Riots ensued and arrests followed. Counterfeit Apple stores appeared in Kunming, China; even the employees thought they were working for Apple, whose lawyers along with Chinese authorities forced the bogus boutiques to shut their doors. Foxcomm suffered the scrutiny of fair trade activists, employee insurrection and abundant bad press. China's foray bidding on rare earths mining in Greenland caught the media's attention. A messy murder trial coincided with revelations about how corrupt national politics is, especially stinging at a time of leadership succession. Anti-Japan demonstrations fueled by dispute over contested islands. And factories are shutting in the face of slowing growth. It hasn't stopped Dreamworks from pushing into the Chinese market, or James Cameron to establish his 3D ventures there. But the obstacles to doing business in the Middle Kingdom remain both cultural and structural.

Ambivalence, thy name is **India**. Dramatic wealth-creation and a burgeoning middle class meant 20% growth in the luxury segment in 2011. Signature perfumes, name initials on t-shirts, personally monogramed watch faces and handbags were all the rage, as if personalization had not been a part of local culture before. But the growth rate has fallen, with the state borrowing too much, inflation high, all in the face of ingrained graft, corruption and red tape. There's still no popular consensus, endless feuding and overlapping bureaucracies overseeing a growing population of more than 1.3 billion. Things that work in India are independent or bypass the state. Feeble growth projected for the next 3-5 years.

A 3-piece punk girl band called Pussy Riot kept **Russia** in the headlines, focusing attention on the redistribution of wealth to a small group of oligarchs, political repression and the clampdown on free speech.

Booming **Brazil** parties on below the equator, with a vibrant economy, a prime lab for new product creation. 70% of the 200 million population is under 26 years of age, the next generation of global consumers. A shortage of skilled labor motivated the state to launch a program which sends 100,000 students to study abroad. For the present, a stable government presides over the economic powerhouse, and life is a *carnaval* in the land of the future.

"When people say it's not about money, it's about money."
– H. L. Mencken

and the moribund

In the **UK**, purple-shirted brand enforcement police deployed out over London during the Olympics, mandated to ferret out ambush marketing of the IOC brand. They sought instances where businesses trod on the exclusive rights of official patrons like Adidas, McDonalds, Coke and BP, who had paid over $2.1 billion in sponsorship money. Of course there were unenforceable near-violations. Nike's ad campaign featured sporting heroics in other Londons throughout the world and Dr. Dre sent unsanctioned headsets to athletes who tweeted about the product during the games. By far the most inventive workaround was a London formalwear shop who proudly advertised in their windows **London 2102 Olympics**, and a 5-square knockoff of the signature ring configuration. The losers were the butcher, whose sausage rings, and the baker, whose bagel rings were cited. Thankfully, no candlestick maker violations reported.

Aux barricades

After a year of activity by the **Occupy** movement, search engines report increased interest in terminology about human rights and democracy. Words and groupings with "inequality" and "struggle" get more inquiries. **Julian Assange** moved in at Ecuador's London embassy, seeking political asylum, relieving boredom by sharing tea and cakes with a succession of celebrity guests. The **FBI** shut down Megaupload as New Zealand busted self-styled "Baron IP" **Kim Dotcom** and seized $50 million in assets, servers and 18 domain names.

"I like to entice people to make mistakes." – Rajat Verma

Take a tablet and call me in the morning

In late October **Microsoft** will launch Surface, an ultra-thin touch-sensitive laptop, challenging market leader iPad, which has significantly purloined sales from low-end desktop computers. This in the face of HP's tablet failure (slower than your mobile phone, 7 weeks on the market, then withdrawn) and Samsung's Galaxy (brand confusion and sloppy app consciousness). Can a skinny laptop running Windows 8 with a touchscreen do the job better than Apple's cash cow ($6.6bn quarterly revenue)? Windows only earned $4.6bn last quarter. The bonus opportunity: a share of the billion phone and tablet downloads already sold in 2012.

"I think of it as a well-known twin brother." – Steven P. Jobs, on celebrity

Three years ago nobody had heard of her

Wonder how **she** has done it? A draconian brand strategy, micromanaging the details. Shorter social media posts, constant status updates, lots of photos, a more inclusive and welcoming posture than rival Rihanna. Confessional letters written in a personal tone and revealing home videos. New album title? Insists that media run it in all-caps. New fragrance, expected to earn $100 million in the first year? Ads suggest if you splash it on, men will be climbing all over you. Accused of wearing fur? "For the press and such who are writing about whether my fur is real or not, please don't forget to credit the designer HERMÈS." Polaroid endorsement deal? Oh, that was so last year.

The luxury category

Valentino's valiant attempt at a virtual museum didn't go down well with critics, who found the slow-loading site, clunky and old media-like, lacking the vitality which internet tools can deliver. It was seen as more of an archive than an experience.

Private jet travel recovered, but not because of disposable income or prestige. Busy executives are booking short hops to circumvent inconvenient connections to secondary cities. The commercial schedule is grossly inefficient to people whose time is more valuable than money.

Missoni made a brilliant partnership with **Target**, whose servers crashed from unanticipated demand on the first day that product was available. People waited in line at big city stores, and shelves emptied in 24 hours. A total win, introducing millions of new customers from the world of mass-market exposed to the idea of limited edition goods, a huge rise in visibility, and improved brand perception for the American retailer.

Louis Vuitton acquired an 18th century mansion in Grasse to house their fragrance creator, in anticipation of re-entering the perfume market. Luxury guru Philippe Mihailovich observed that they "bought themselves an instant heritage for any new creations they will launch."

trendseekers alerts

The dinosaur

It's the Internet, stupid. Or more accurately, the stupid Internet, its own worst enemy. As the marketplace hungers for a real-time web, developers struggle to update archaic technology that wasn't built to support mobile or video, especially new gaming which eats over 90% of all bandwidth. The kicker: it's leaky, meaning the very platform which has changed your life seriously compromises your privacy and security.

Never the twain

The greatest dilemma for online businesses is to reconcile with the offline universe. And vice versa. Etailers begin to explore the click and brick concept. Amazon, eBay and Google have opened storefronts, to leverage human interaction in more intimate levels of engagement than possible online. It's evidence of a renewed focus on personal relationships with customers.

Trading on feelings

Customer Experience Management (CEM) strategies promote intimacy between brands and shoppers. Brands now rush to re-establish bonds with their customer base. **GoDaddy**, a web domain registry, uses hot girls as its signature marketing device. Its founder does a video blog surrounded by skimpily-clad babes, who also appear in its ad campaign. The strategy did not appear to adversely affect a $2.25 billion IPO. Nor did reports of the CEO big-game-hunting endangered species in Africa, after which the company claimed an uptick in sales. **Google Chrome**'s new ad campaign doesn't focus on product or features, it's all about emotions. After testing a dozen commercial spots on the Internet, Google ran the ad that had the most views, not "likes".

Touching immortality

Google's latest perks extend into the afterlife for 34,000 qualifying employees. Die on the job and your spouse receives 50% of your annual income for the next decade, all stock vested immediately, and kids get $1000 a month until age 19. A backhanded strategy to improve retention and performance, increase happiness, creativity and productivity. And please, nobody mention the upcoming anti-trust suit the Justice Department is mounting.

"Fuck Google. Ask me." – t-shirt worn by Parisian youth in Gare du Nord, October 2011

Social irony

In the face of increased mobile user consumption, **Facebook** had no revenue strategy, effectively killing Farmville, a hugely popular casual game. Their much-touted IPO turned into a free fall, from an opening price of $40/share, crashing to a low of $17.55/share since May. Analysts say the share price could go as low as $10. Confidence ebbs when people stop believing the story. Triple-digit growth of users is history, and Wall Street's hope for "a paradigm-breaking" value perception evaporated. The majority of users are women, who make more posts and uploads, and show higher rates of participation. A Facebook addicts rehab support group launched its own page, after which it received 3,000 "likes".

Yelp posts are seen to help small businesses, but to decrease revenue in chain restaurants, an important advertiser category.

"If I am a legend, then why am I so lonely?"
– attributed to Judy Garland

Reputation crushed

Oblivious to the passionate discussion on all sides concerning customer experience, **PayPal** suffered the consequences following an imbroglio over a violin valued at $2500. Seller shipped the WWII era heirloom to buyer in Canada. Buyer didn't like the product, claimed it was counterfeit. Often violins are of dodgy provenance, dubious labeling. It's illegal to ship counterfeit goods, so PayPal ordered buyer to destroy the disputed item and provide evidence of it. Insisted seller refund the money to buyer. Seller lost the product and the sale, buyer got a refund but not the item they wanted, and the only winner appeared to be PayPal. Until the media heard about it. Ten months later the unsatisfying not-transaction still comes up on web searches.

Momentum lost

The reservoir of goodwill **Netflix** built with their $1 million crowdsourcing prize brought a better search and recommendation algorithm. Then it all went zap! in a matter of a month. A million subscribers defected after the DVD-by-mail rental business announced a price increase and the concurrent launch of 'Quikster', a streaming sub-brand with a confusing add-on pricing offer. "We became a symbol of the evil, greedy corporation," CEO Reed Hasting said. "Then we faced a reputational hit that created significantly more cancellations than we anticipated." By August the share price had plummeted, even as streaming subscriber numbers grew.

Au revoir

Jack LaLanne, who singlehandedly invented the health food and exercise craze in the USA, did his final reps; he swam handcuffed to Alcatraz every year on his birthday into his eighties. **Madame Nhu**, an Evita-like dragon lady of the Vietnam War, went to the great re-education camp in the sky after 40 years of luxurious exile. **Eva Zeisel**, famous for Jetson-style atomic age ceramics and dinnerware, set her last table. **Kodak** faded away, a heritage name who never quite processed how the digital imaging revolution developed. In its final chapter, **Barnes & Noble** was murdered by Amazons.

the following touchpoints to debate and discussion for the coming year

"You are free to do anything, as long as it involves shopping."
– Slavoj Žižek

Just wave your handheld at it

More than half US customers own smartphones. eBay predicts $10 billion a year in mobile transactions by end of 2013. Starbucks and Square partnered on integrated mobile transactions which are simple, fast, focused on the customer (meaning extensive data capture), on a massive scale. They hope to create a compelling, safe experience for shoppers. People always choose convenience and don't realize the cost of privacy, yet security remains a critical concern. Luckily, the market will be fragmented for the next 2 years, as the real shakedown of adoption, demand and technology occurs.

"They do not know it, but they are doing it." – Karl Marx, *Das Capital*

Cyberinsecurity

The elephant in the room is called cyberattacks. Sony had 100 million customer accounts compromised in 2011 at a cost of $200 million, followed by 58 class action suits. You know it's serious when Deloitte & Fowler say that social media risks are "on par with financial risks." Companies can be decimated by breaches of confidentiality, fast-spreading malicious rumors, financial disclosures. Insurance against these kind of threats now a growth category, fertile markets for policies which cover the twin risks of privacy and security.

News from the offplanet

Privatization knows its priorities. SpaceX, a commercial enterprise, carried ice cream to the International Space Station on their Dragon vehicle's maiden flight. Also ported 2000 lbs. of other critical supplies. The company will soon deliver room-temperature astronauts in a 4-seat passenger capsule.

Please stay away
Too early for place re-branding: Syria, Libya, Yemen, Venezuela, Haiti, North Korea

"You said you were a mushroom, now jump into the basket." – Russian proverb

Terminology and concepts entering the mainstream

Fetishistic disavowal - a tendency to retain a behavior or action as a hedge, even if one does not believe in it

Freemium - a risky online business strategy which involves giving away a game and then charging for the extra features

Mac Lust - compulsive need for newest generation device

Metcalfe's Law - the value of a telecommunications network is proportional to the square of the number of connected users of the system

Narquitecture - the grandiose building style favored by Latin American drug barons

Nomophobia - the fear of being without a phone

Overgeneral memory - a tendency to recall past events in a broad, vague manner

Socioemotional selectivity - clinical term for defriending

What is a brand?

When I told a skeptical friend that a brand is a mythology, the remark immediately elicited resistance. I insisted, "There's a heroic component we attach to our idea of brands, and we expect them to behave according to our personal ideals."

Thanks to those who contributed the following definitions to the discussion:

"A brand is the intangible aspect of a tangible thing." - Massimo Vignelli

Massimo, a legend of international graphic design, created the much-heralded NYC subway map. While graphics provide a synthetic interpretation of brand, the idea proposed here suggests abstract engagement vital to its success.

"A brand is what reduces uncertainties, generating attraction by association." - Cristián Saracco

Madrid-based Cristián leads Brand 3.0, a 10,000 member practitioner network. His idea carries the concept of community-creation as critical to clarifying the branding process.

"A brand is only as solid as the next customer engagement." - Patrick Harris

Patrick heads thoughtengine, a London consultancy. His definition reflects a customer-centric view of branding. Without the customer, there would be no brand.

"A brand is belief." - Tom Hulme

Tom is a Project Manager for IDEO in London. His view of a brand has to do with the idea of advocacy as paramount.

Recently I have thought about brands as imaginary compacts. A brand is created in the mind. It's weightless and invisible, and our relationships with brands live purely in the realm of the intellectual. Thus an individual's commitment to a brand is unilateral and exists only in a conceptual space. A brand becomes part of our unique cosmology.

2011

"Always behave as if nothing had happened, no matter what has happened." –Arnold Bennett

"Find any reason." – Marketing slogan painted on Goan wall

I'm late this year in writing to you, and I probably need some quantitative easing. From December through March I circled the globe in a cloud of WikiLeaks fallout. B of A, MasterCard, Visa, eBay and PayPal had long ceased to process contribution payments to what some hoped were bold, righteous revolutionaries. Apple banned an online donation app in response to the disclosures of the aspiring journalistic entity. I went to Milan to look at muddled new visual branding for WikiLeaks by Metahaven, a Netherlands-based design company working for free in a grand gesture of anti-monetizing. Words I wrote in December were obsolete by February. By the end of March a new term, The Arab Spring, had emerged.

I began to wonder if brands as well mimic the cycles of life: they incubate, are born, rise and die. And new brands are created. I ponder the strange ramifications of all the games with which we are distracted. In Ancient Rome, games were staged to pacify the population.

update on last year's hot topics

Upstarts

Economists now predict a bubble of risk for emerging markets as investors rush in. They simply can't say when the crash occurs. Capital inflow peaks often precede crises.

The IHT's annual luxury conference heads to São Paulo in November 2011, a telling indicator of where the smart money is placing its bets. Suzy Menkes asked, "Who is not drawn, in the current chilly financial climate, to a place where ... a steaming economy and an opulent upper class combine to create an enthusiasm – rarely now seen in the western world – for fine goods... [and] explosive growth is guaranteed..." With 62% of its population under 29, Brazil is the perfect consumer laboratory for youth brands. Youth culture is world culture.

Then there's the run-up to the Olympics. Even the legendary Pelé has voiced his concerns that facilities won't be ready. The Commonwealth Games in Delhi all over again?

Brazil reports success with 'conditional cash transfers' where individuals receive funds if certain requirements are met. In the last six years, the income of poor has grown 7 times faster than income of rich, but the separation of wealth is still profound. Early in 2010, the Brazilian investment firm 3G Capital struck a deal to buy Burger King for about $4 billion. Another Brazilian firm, JBS tried to offer $12.5 billion for Sara Lee, hoping to score attractive assets like the coffee business, growing brands in Western Europe and Brazil. No transaction occurred, due to disputes over sale price since the brand carries so much debt. A consortium of companies upped the ante successfully blocking the deal.

Wonder who China's 2010 political BFs were? These pre-uprising nations boycotted the controversial Nobel ceremony: Afghanistan, Algeria, Colombia, Cuba, Egypt, Iran, Iraq, Kazakhstan, Morocco, Pakistan, the Philippines, Russia, Saudi Arabia, Serbia, Sudan, Tunisia, Ukraine, Venezuela, and Vietnam.

Inexplicably, some years ago after they helped China build its Great Firewall, Cisco got an innovation award from the US State Department. Li-Ning sport shoes has a 5-year plan to establish its brand in the USA, going toe-to-toe with Nike, possible candidate for a comparable accolade in the Middle Kingdom?

Unprecedented prosperity has China experiencing a boom in domestic and outbound tourism. These could be the same folks supporting a massive trade in endangered animals in Asia, consuming bear bile, tiger paws, rhino horns. Blame it on the rising middle class. China makes 80% of counterfeit goods globally, last yearly estimate (2007) $250bn. It's more than just handbags. Also critical components like brake pads, everyday consumer goods like toothpaste, music, movies, games, software, aircraft engine parts, ball bearings, pharmaceuticals, electronics. China's policing of the Internet for pornography or political content raises questions why it doesn't do the same for sites that offer pirated or counterfeit goods. Shut down those guys and you affect China's counterfeit industry, which employs millions of workers, distributors, shop clerks. It's so huge and corrupt that authorities routinely tip off shops about impending raids. Triads in China deeply involved. China also plays its part in international distribution networks. You may be looking at what claims to be a Canadian pharmacy, when in fact the drugs are manufactured in India, the site is run out of China and your payment is going to another group in Russia. "Nothing sells like replicas," says a counterfeit bag dealer.

"La vérité, l'âpre vérité." ("The truth, the harsh truth")
– Georges Danton

China and Asia are the leading growth markets for Chateau Haut-Brion. China ordered Airbus aircraft valued at $15bn. Club Med is managing a huge expansion in China, presently the company's second biggest market outside France. Renault, previously navigating morale problems and suicides, fired three execs and filed suit against two of them, at first rumored to be over transfer of electric car and battery technology to Chinese companies. The French eventually backed down, citing their own internal troubles, paying off the disabused execs.

Meanwhile, China and India pledged to increase trade to $100bn a year, but probably not in broadcast media. India's already addicted to reality TV, 700 million mobile phone subscribers vote on talent show winners. Vodafone has backed off despoiling the landscape with its logos, while competitor Airtel rushed in, capitalizing on the economies of *cognitive fluency*, borrowing a trick from the playbook of Louis Vuitton's repeat LV pattern, hijacking Vodafone's visual brand by recklessly plastering its similar redesigned red signature on any available surface. Investors are shunning India after the Commonwealth Games and fallout over telecom licenses sold at bargain prices to bribe-payers.

HSBC announced it is quitting retail banking in Russia- too much state-owned competition. BP is still trying to salvage their oil deal with Rosneft.

and the moribund

In 1991, economists were predicting that Japan would overtake the USA as the world's largest economy by 2010. Prior to the earthquake, tsunami and nuclear crisis, after a generation of deflation and extreme debt burden, living standards were crumbling along with Japan's economy. A symptom: "microhouses", tiny homes on miniscule plots of land were all the rage, symbolic of a dark, subdued vision for the future. The luxury category evaporated. A pervasive pessimism had taken hold, especially among the young, who were regarded as a generation of consumption-haters living in a time of collapsed demand, consumers refusing to consume, corporations holding back on investments and banks sitting on cash. By the time this group hit their 60s their frugality was expected to cost the Japanese economy $420bn. Oddly, hope has returned to Japanese youth. Many unemployed grads have moved into the relief effort, volunteering their time. The unexpected byproduct of tragedy is a rebirth of optimism and sense of purpose.

Fewer than 2 million people use Facebook in Japan.

And why are Takashi Murakami's cutesy characters so popular as an export commodity? Could be brilliant licensing lawyers, cheerful colors, shiny surfaces, industrial precision or a not-so-subtle subtext of sexuality.

"Toil, envy, want, the patron, and the jail." –Dr. Johnson, on the poet's life

---

Despite the arrival of the economic day of reckoning, Americans still have a greater tolerance for capitalism's creative destruction. New product creation and innovation, a willingness to fail, and openness to entrepreneurial endeavor may eventually daunt the doomsayers. Foreign students still want to study in the US. They like a more flexible curriculum, the international student community, and a less theoretical and more practical approach to education. They prefer an environment sympathetic to diversity and a borderless global view. Besides, who wants to study in a place like London, with its depressing weather, higher cost of living, and cold climate?

Oh, most inglorious quantification

Thus far, 5.2 million volumes have been digitized for the Google Books project, 500 billion words. You can now browse cultural trends throughout history as recorded in print, analyze cultural influences statistically. A Harvard post-doc has done research to demonstrate how vast digital databases can transform our understanding of language, culture and the flow of ideas. Research guys, take note: here's a new way to measure the endurance of fame, track celebrity. They've already figured out that notoriety rises and fades twice as fast as it did 100 years ago, an answer derived by surveying verb use, changes in grammar, evolution of language. Heretofore there's been resistance to quantitative analysis in some corners of the humanities, but it turns out Andy Warhol was right.

Show me the money

News Corp attracted 105,000 paying customers for web versions of The Times and Sunday Times of London, despite first estimating that site visits would drop by 90%. Initially the visits fell by only 42%, then 93%, far short of publishers' hopes that it might someday replace dwindling print ad revenue. The Financial Times attracted 189,000 paying customers for its web site, which uses a metered model limiting number of free articles before more charges kick in. In April 2011 the NYTimes did the same. The IHT is giving away its iPad app, but not for long. Regional papers are developing hyperlocal sites, accumulation of small-traffic locally-based news stations. Visits are increasing tenfold, but still not profitable. Another cost-saving measure: automated news-generating algorithms, no human writers needed.

The hottest, fastest ebooks growth category in the USA is romance novels. Might be a clue for the news media: boost online revenues with more stories about stereotypes, true love and triumphant heroic behavior.

"A likely impossibility is always preferable to an unconvincing possibility." –Aritstotle, on tragedy

Social media

Twitter chugs onward, the ultimate disposable media. By the end of July, the 20 billionth tweet had posted. It took four years to reach the 10 billionth tweet, less than 5 months to double it. Charlie Sheen set a new world record in 2011, gaining 1 million tweet followers in a single day.

Last August, outgoing Google boss Eric Schmidt told the WSJ he feared people did not understand the consequences of having so much information about themselves online. He suggested people may need to change their names in order to escape their previous online activity. "We know roughly who you are, roughly what you care about, roughly who your friends are."

Marketers lost interest in MySpace, much like Rupert Murdoch did when he got distracted buying the *Wall Street Journal* and discontinued regular visits to their office downstairs. An eloquent death knell tolled when the January 12 *New York Times* referred to MySpace as "a slightly tawdry online backwater". It mattered not that the website was redesigned to focus on entertainment for Gen Y people 13 to 35 years old, constantly updating, focusing on luring active users with virtual badges in a rewards-driven scenario, trying to become relevant again. The concept was to recapture a position in social entertainment, act as a niche player, capitalize on long staying power. With a paltry 120 million users primarily listening to music and sharing info and opinions, ad spending was still projected to decline to 60% of prior year's numbers, a trifling $300m. Myspace ads reach about 24% of US online users (Facebook reaches 62%, with ad revenue expected to soar to $2 billion in the same time period.) Myspace even hired a former Facebook exec, who left after a disappointing 10 months. Murdoch is banking on the low start-up cost of his iPad venture, *The Daily,* to capture a chunk of business from the hot new Apple platform.

Harrisburg University of Science and Technology, an 800-student college in Pennsylvania, declared a temporary blackout of social media on campus, blocking Twitter and Facebook. Inexplicably, respondents reported better classroom concentration during the weeklong ban.

Brilliant new business idea: look up before you hook up. For a fee, a clutch of start-up services will prescreen people you meet over the net before you disclose any sensitive personal information to them.

First touted as season's hottest movie, people lost interest in "The Social Network" and it underperformed at the domestic box office and failed to ignite in the national mind. Still swept the Golden Globes, an industry award usually acknowledging profitability rather than quality.

"We have a policy of ambiguity." –Mossad, re 2010 Dubai hit squad caught on surveillance video

Celebrity

Johnny Depp and Angelina Jolie, considered among Hollywood's most bankable stars, saw their film "The Tourist" fizzle on release, earning about $17 million box office the first week. The film cost $175 million to make and market. Sony Pictures Entertainment acknowledged soft sales but said expected overseas theatrical reception to be "substantially stronger." Break-even could come after DVD sales and broadcast licensing.

Yet, it's largely an ambiguous process trying to quantify star power. There are too many ratings systems in play, and they indicate sharply differing results. Most address only awareness and affinity. The info vendors suggest faster polling results, but that's flash-in-the-pan thinking and might not be reliable. Other research pundits propose wider polling of attributes like buzz and media attention, but they only survey media junkies. And online polls may be unrepresentative because only a select group opts in.

Belated congratulations to Jim Morrison, pardoned posthumously by Florida clemency board for 1967 indecent exposure charge.

Who gets more Google hits than Barack Obama? Justin Bieber. Adolescent girls flocked to his new 3D concert movie, a career launched by YouTube posts. The kid had a hard trip to Israel; he just wanted to sing but he kept getting roped into political agendas and he mostly stayed in his hotel room ducking the world's pushiest paparazzi.

Who's the biggest instant celebrity-creator in the USA, who concurrently influences your soft drink preference? Look in the direction of News Corp. *XFactor* is sponsored by Pepsi, *American Idol* is sponsored by Coke, both Fox reality TV shows emanating from the same producers. And Piers Morgan, taking over Larry King's slot, was judge on *America's Got Talent*. Connect the dots and it spells Rupert Murdoch guiding your FMCG brand affinities.

"Wherefore wealth, if not to purchase pleasure?"
–John Blake White, 1812

The luxury category

Rolls Royce sold 2711 cars in 2010, sales up 171%. If Asia is so hot for luxury sales, then why does the USA remain the brand's #1 market? Established dealership base, largest community of loyal owners willing to trade up, and launch of Rolls' newest 'affordable' model.

Ferrari holds to its classy routine for delivery of a new vehicle. Once the purchase is a done deal the buyer's measurements are taken for custom seats. Months later, when the car is ready to be collected, the proud owner attends a private reception at the Ferrari plant. All the people from the assembly team line up, there's a ceremonial transfer of keys, confetti gets tossed, the factory doors are thrown open and the happy driver cruises the car out onto a private track for the first spin.

When Richemont acquired commerce site Net-A-Porter for half a billion dollars, nobody blinked. The site gets 4 million visitors a month. It's no secret that fancy shoes, diamond rings, cars, eyewear are now actively sold online.

Strangest co-branding of the year: DKNY and Veuve Cliquot partnering in boots.

Arnaut hopes to win his bid for Hermès by a war of attrition, but his purchase of Bulgari slid through effortlessly. The Italian jewelry brand, languishing for years, already shows improved profits from LVMH's vast category expertise.

Want to spend the night at the Château de Versailles? A luxury renovation of the Hôtel du Grand Contrôle into a 23-room boutique property is in progress. Cost for a night: a paltry €600, plus every room has a view of l'Orangerie.

A growing investor base from mainland China and India is stoking a heated market for investment-grade colored stones. One consequence has been the rise in price of medium-quality diamonds, fueled by new buyers from China, HK, Singapore, Taiwan and elsewhere in the region. The world's rarest gems traditionally went to a clientele of celebrities, royal families, wealthy Middle Easterners, and a growing base of Asian and Russian customers. Diamond prices are relatively stable compared to other auction items, even with newly popular colors like brown, chocolate, cognac, honey, clove and cinnamon. Over the years, based on their extreme rarity, blue diamonds have seen their prices rise dramatically.

PPR divested of Conforama a midmarket furniture brand. They are hovering around Burberry, currently valued at $1.5bn, who reported strong improvement in quarterly earnings owing to excellent growth in –surprise- Asia. PPR already owns Gucci, Balenciaga, Golf Warehouse, Puma. It's part of Pinault/Artemis' aggressive strategy to refocus brand in the luxury, sports and lifestyle sectors. PPR bought Volcom in April 2011, adding the established and irreverent youth boardsports brand to its portfolio.

trendseekers alerts

Au revoir

Benoit Mandelbrot left his body in October. He coined the term "fractal" to refer to a new class of mathematical shapes whose uneven contours could mimic the irregularities found in nature. He used the geometry of fractals to explain how galaxies cluster, how wheat prices change over time, how mammalian brains fold as they grow. He said he preferred to 'stimulate the field by making bold and crazy conjectures," then move on before his claims had been verified. And see ya later, baby, to **Robert B. Parker** who penned over 20 volumes about Spenser ("spelled like the poet") a tough-talking Boston private eye and perpetual softie with perhaps the most annoying girlfriend in contemporary literature. He always tells you what he is wearing, cooking and eating. Parker extended the brand to movies, young adult novels and a hit television series. Gazillions of copies in print.

Now it's graphics.

Mobile, location and photo may have VC's favorite buzz words last year, but with increasing numbers of gamers using mobile devices, the visual performance of chips is suddenly of greatest interest. According to some forecasts, video will account for about 90% of all consumer internet traffic by 2013.

Cognitive fluency. Say it thrice.

There's new validation that the myth of eyeballs is no myth at all. Scientists now begin to understand the extent with which fluency guides our thinking, even when we don't know it is at work. When your agency tells you they can guarantee number of visual impressions, Facebook friends, clickthroughs, it's true the technique works. You will get noticed. But at what cost to the landscape or the manipulation of the unwitting in the interest of selling product? If growth is all you care about, then go ahead. Despoil the landscape, pummel people into mindless submission, but don't forget to tell them how much you care about their wellbeing, sustainability and preserving the beauty of planet earth.

All a big game

Whole lotta playing going on, including the birth if a new category, casual gaming, which you're supposed to do while you wait in line at the bank, or sit in the doctor's office, on a bus bench, typical session lasting less than 15 minutes. The hot commodity includes Angry Birds which you are soon to see everywhere, licensed products like stuffed toys, the movie, every digital venue possible. Nobody noticed the reference to a war between Avian Flu and Swine flu. 50 million download later, Rovio, the Finnish manufacturer, says people around the world rack up 200 million minutes of game play every day.

Two influence peddlers bought into the category: Google acquired Slide, a gaming firm; Disney released "Classic Mickey" an artful failure with glaring interface problems, and remade "Tron", a movie about a video game.

Redken created "Busy Scissors" a hairstyling and simulation game for the Nintendo Wii, aimed at girls 8 to 16. Designed to make women want to go to the salon again instead of buying products for home use. The product underperformed because it didn't have a social networking component. "Fate of the World" enabled you to save or destroy the planet, using climate prediction models, with change achieved by applying policies. Players can take the authoritarian route, or darker options like sending secret agents to overthrow recalcitrant governments, surreptitiously adding contraceptives to the water supply of nations resistant to birth control, even release a genetically engineered virus to crash the world population. It only proves human beings have a natural fascination with destruction and chaos, validated by the eagerly awaited "Call of Duty Black Ops". It garnered $650 million in sales in its first five days of release, after development costs of less than $30 million.

Thirsty for love

Coca-Cola made a splendid decision to build up the mango juice industry in Haiti after the earthquake, supporting 25,000 farmers. They missed an opportunity to send an informative message about choosing biodegradable footwear when they decorated their 2011 cans with flip-flops, a global pollution nightmare once discarded.

Talk about conflicted

The premise: bundle good hardware with services. Nokia now focuses this idea on some of the world's poorest consumers. Since 2009, 6.3 million people have signed up to pay Nokia for commodity data in India, China and Indonesia. Most of all cell phones sold there are simpler models, capable of little more than text messaging. Of the globe's 4.6 billion mobile users, two thirds live in emerging markets. Nokia is the market leader with 34% share, but need to attract the next generation of upwardly mobile phone users. They need to create tremendous brand loyalty- nobody else in the market is providing data and hardware. The partnership with Microsoft for Windows Phone 7 might add to the leverage.
Concurrently, at the high end, Nokia is suing Apple, alleging 13 of its patents for touch screens were used without permission.

the following touchpoints to debate and discussion for the coming year

Altruism gene

Studies at the University of Bonn identified the difference in a single gene associated with increased willingness to donate. The gene, COMT-Val variant, contains building instructions for an enzyme which switches off certain messengers in the brain, the most well-known being dopamine. In studies, student guinea pigs donated twice as much more to hypothetical causes. Dopamine is involved in controlling social behavior, and is associated with the neuropeptide vasopressin, linked to positive emotionality. Fundraisers for NGOs, take note.

Trendy color therapy

Need a pick me up at a time when many people have had their fill of misfortune? Leatrice Eiseman, a color psychologist and director of Pantone's color institute for 25 years believes there's an innate optimism in this year's color of the year, Honeysuckle Pink. She says the idea is to get consumers to say, "Oh, neat color. Maybe I need to buy those plates." Two years ago consumers were recoiling and sought traditional heritage looks during the recession. Colors went earthy, people needed relief after several years of depressing economic news and bland colors. Chili Pepper was the color of 2007, coincidentally the last year of the economic boom, applied to clothes, cameras, plates, chairs. Whom do you believe? In November the Color Marketing Group convened in Portland, Oregon and projected that Honeymoon, a warm, mustardy goldish shade of yellow would be the big color of 2011. A good time to reconsider the color of the sweater you just bought at GAP.

Pay more attention at work

What's interesting here is that lower productivity should actually reduce short term unemployment, because companies have to hire more workers to do the same amount of work. Normally productivity slows and shifts into reverse when recessions hit, as companies cut output faster than they shed workers. If productivity slows here in the US, wage growth is likely to be anemic. These days companies add workers only when absolutely necessary.
Certain jobs are gone forever. Your receptionist turned into a doorbell and intercom.

News from the offplanet

In December, SpaceX, a commercial company, successfully launched a space capsule into orbit and recovered the capsule on its return to Earth. The company claimed their achievement would create a paradigm shift in the U.S. launch industry and reinvigorate a sagging space economy. Elon Musk's original investment of $100 million led to the NASA SpaceX development contract worth $278 million. The big prize: a cargo delivery contract worth $1.6 billion. This all happened eight years after Musk founded the company. Now the Dragon capsule is being readied to ferry U.S. astronauts to the International Space Station.

But the state of New Mexico, ravaged by debt, searches for additional private investors for their Spaceport USA, still under construction. A second 2-mile runway remains incomplete, original managers have been replaced and the project put on hold while the search for more money goes forward. The port was designed to handle Virgin's first suborbital flights in 2012, a thrill ride which costs $200,000 per person and features 4 minutes of weightlessness.

China's proceeding with work on their own space station, about 1/3 the weight of the ISS. They plan to use it as an orbiting research base and halfway house, intending to land a man on the Moon by 2025.

Please stay away

A strange year for place branding. Chile rescued its miners for around $120 million in costs, then gained incredible nation brand value, attention and regard in the world arena, including high grades from economist Jeffrey Sachs for its progressive economic policies. Nobody mentioned reports of genocide on Easter Island over indigenous peoples' territorial claims.

The Styria province in SE Austria, an area bordering Hungary and Slovenia, saw a mini-boom generated by 14 mayors working together to develop a hybrid business strategy called Vulkanland. The regional project promotes local, green, self-sustaining businesses, with the help of EEC money. The unintended complication: Hardly any houses on the market, a reverse anti-branding which keeps people from moving there.

The Arab Spring decimated tourism in Egypt and Morocco, Multiple disasters in Japan, natch, Tunisia, not going there.

Bahrain, crossing it off the list. Syria, ask again next year. It makes you wonder if the fundamentalists are laundering money by secretly investing in catastrophe bonds.

Brand resurrection

All eyes on the marriage of Fiat and Chrysler. Let's hope the new 500 built in Mexico for the US market is the next PT Cruiser.

"You blocks, you stones, you worse than senseless things!" – **Shakespeare, from *Julius Caesar***

Terminology and concepts entering the mainstream in 2011:

Connection technologies - digital media which allows largely unrestricted sharing of photos and information.

Degrowth- A hot new movement which challenges conventional notions of sustainability.

Dresser savings - The piles of cash that people keep at home for fear that their banks may –yet again- go bankrupt.

Grass mud horse - a mythical creature that has become a protest symbol against Internet censorship in China.

Great Firewall - China's sophisticated system which blocks large amounts of information from entering the country over the Internet.

Knightian uncertainty - the idea that there is a distinction between risks to which you can assign probabilities, and uncertainties which you just cannot fathom.

Online disinhibition effect - what happens when people often change their behavior in radical ways over the net. Anonymity increases potential for unethical conduct.

Pay walls - revenue models erected around online digital content so that news media companies can monetize web editions.

PIIGS virus - the failure of Portugal, Ireland, Italy, Greece and Spain to use years of cheap credit and fast growth to create durable economies. The not-BRICs syndrome.

Range anxiety- The fear of running out of electricity and getting stranded because all electric cars cannot go as far as conventional ones.

Retargeting- a commercial surveillance system that follows consumers based on online browsing where a sale did not result.

Theta spikes- electrical activity in the brain indicating fatigue, often an index related to extreme information overload

Trolling- the act of posting inflammatory, derogatory or provocative messages in public forums

Upcycling- turning waste into products of greater value

"Thunder occurs when clouds collide." –Anaxagoras

What is a brand?

This year I'll share some random jottings from my own notebooks.

A brand is a crutch to adoption. My friend Patrick Harris said this in passing last August during his presentation at the Medinge meeting. If that's the case, then a brand can sometimes act as an aid to an inadequate entity. This implies that brands exist to support a weak case for adoption.

A brand is the voice of the future. A brand is often are consumed by its past. We need to remember there's a big difference between regressive behavior and heritage values. In the commercial arena one must look forward, over the horizon.

A brand is a polyglot. It speaks the local language. This lesson has already been learned in the emerging economies. Brands are transportable, as long as they can be understood.

A brand is how I differentiate myself from you and how I identify with you. Here is stated the fundamental ambiguity. I both express commonality and individuality with the brands I advocate.

A contrarian brand is always fresh.

No matter who else originated it, or to whom it belongs, you always say The Brand Is Me.

Thanks to those who contributed the following definitions:

"A brand is whatever creates an irrational preference for itself."
- Aditya Nath Jha
Aditya ,formerly Head of Global Brand and Communication at Infosys Technology in Bangalore, is now developing a new venture in the digital animation category. I like the idea of a brand as a wild catalyst to the product experience. How does a fixed commodity provoke spontaneity?

"A brand begins as a story, carrying you along with it. It lifts you away from your normal life as you buy into the vision, and later you bring back a part of the dream."
– Virginia James
Virginia is London-based Style Director for Next, an apparel brand. Fantasy and narrative are integral to our ideas concerning clothing. Virginia's vision has to do with a brand built around the idea of imagination.

"A brand is a means to communicate the organization's internal truth."
– Enric Bernal
Enric is a principal at Pinea3 in Barcelona. Much of Pinea3's workshop method deploys tools designed to build self-recognition and actualization.

"A brand is identity revealed"
-Erika Uffindell
Erika heads Uffindell Group in London UK. Identity, by nature, is a mysterious commodity. Perhaps a brand exists to make the arcane understandable.

Recently I have thought about brands as *synthetic realities which need to be made personal*. It's all the more difficult to get close to a brand if a membrane of technology intrudes. We're layers of interpretation away from the essence of the brands we build.

2010

"Everything that deceives can be said to enchant." –Plato

"That is the beauty of branding: brutalized, used like an instrument, it turns against its creator." –Pierre d'Huy

We invest such hope in brands, infusing them with high expectations that no entity short of a deity could meet. We want our brands to behave like gods. We ask our brands to live up to their promises, act sustainably, be responsive and constant, tell the truth, be accommodating, service-driven, transparent, reasonable, economic, culturally sensitive, prescient. We want to dialogue with them, have a conversation, pursue a relationship, expect them to listen when we rage, restore us when things go wrong, and apologise as we show them the door. Thus we place brands into the realm of immortals, seeking an unrealistic perfection in the institutions which we work so hard to build. It's the brand professional's dilemma, where the thresholds of idealism stand. With oversight a given, CSR an expected component of any brand, and the speed at which reputations can be lost, what's a brand to do? It's particularly troubling when marketers talk about powering old prejudices. Those are the practices that got us into so much trouble in gratification-world, encouraged the banks to venture our money in a grossly cavalier manner and market us into record consumer debt. While brands need to stand for contentment and fulfillment, they also need to stand for clear thought and responsible behavior. The next time you bite into a bar of chocolate, sip a cup of coffee, try to decide whether to buy a new iTablet, watch Fox News, sign a 2-year contract with Vodafone, make a deposit at Citibank or splash on some Terre d'Hermès, are you going ask yourself what deeper meanings the gesture supports? It all comes down to the soul-searching question, What does adopting this brand really say about me?

update on last year's hot topics

Emerging economies

It's all big-bigger-biggest numbers in China. Mercedes-Benz agreed to pay up to $100 million for naming rights to a new sports stadium in Shanghai, the first time they have done this outside Germany, part of a collaboration with NBA's huge push there. China's population of wealthy individuals with more than $1 million in investable assets surpassed that of Britain in 2008. In the UK, ultra-wealthy Chinese shoppers now outspend their Russian and Arab counterparts.
China has world's largest population of internet users yet makes fewer online transactions than in America. Many Chinese resisted purchasing online, wary about scams and faulty merchandise. Alibaba launched AliPay, who hold the money in escrow until after the buyer has received the item and confirmed they are satisfied with it. 200 million registered users, doing around $150 million *a day* in transactions.

But for all the rosy economic reports, China is as well a succession of bad-news stories. Take for example, *dysprosium and terbium extraction.* China does serious environmental damage with this "rare earth mining," which accounts for 99% of the world's production. Sustainability alert! These are critical materials for wind turbine technology, and alternative energies. More than half the shipments are smuggled, illegal, unregulated, in an industry dominated by murderous criminal gangs. It sounds like the ore in the movie *Avatar*, right? Unobtainium. After China rolled *out new measures to limit citizens' ability to set up personal web sites or to use hundreds of Internet entertainment services,* Google got seriously hacked and now says it can't operate there: they won't even guarantee "basic service" in the Middle Kingdom.

Oreo is on the fast track to becoming the world's most regionally sensitive cookie brand. Last year sales grew 30% outside the USA. Kraft already sells baked goods in Russia, cookies named for Communist heroes. Now they're considering selling Oreos there. For the Chinese market Kraft created Oreo wafers that are "smaller and less sweet than the traditional version." A new take *on cookie-based profiling.*

Career-savvy women are the movers and shakers behind **India**'s transitionary society. The new age Indian is acquisitive, brand-conscious and wants the best. The reality is that India still has fewer wealthy consumers than Ireland. Mercenary marketers claim it's not about informing a new consciousness, more about powering old prejudices.

Brasil scored the Olympics, and a week later drug gangs shot down a police helicopter over the *favelas* in Rio. The government responded with a paltry $60 million pledge for additional security for the games. It won't go far. There must be some deep correlation: *Avatar*'s most important overseas markets turn out to be Russia and Brasil.

Zegna says **China** will be its biggest market by the end of 2010. Australia and Latin America are regarded as "less mature luxury markets." Top manager at Zegna believes luxury's new frontier is Africa.

Mickey goes to Shanghai

We're in the thick of an Asian theme-park boomlet. Singapore is getting a new Universal park, Malaysia getting Legoland, a $465 million upgrade planned for HK Disney. A bleak near-term picture elsewhere worldwide. Six Flags filed for bankruptcy protection, Dubailand project was supposed to include Paramount, Marvel and Dreamworks, now halted. Japan has an aging population and stagnant economy, with most theme park attendance flat or down. Disney typically relies on the creation of new Disney TV channels to promote its brand abroad, but China's limits on foreign media have made that impossible. The go-ahead for the new Shanghai park did not come with concessions from China on the television front. Analysts believe approval probably came from the prospect of massive job creation. About *300 million potential customers* live within two hours of the park site, which is between the city's airport and downtown.

P&G plots for new markets

It's the McElroy memo all over again, but with a colonialist twist. In order to meet re-org targets, P&G needs to add around a half million new customers every day for the next five years, outside their traditional markets. To do so they hope to attract new customers in places like Nigeria, India and Somalia. Rivals Unilever and Colgate have established presences in these markets, such a foothold that they are known as "walled cities" in the FMCG industry. But P&G believes there is room for competition. While they don't expect $110 a year per capita, like US consumers spend, they hope for levels like Mexico's $20 a year. Currently China is at less than $3 a year, so do the math. But, wait- customers in emerging markets have little money to spend. P&G will have to crack the intricacies of distribution, and adjust their products into smaller and cheaper sizes. One interesting metric is holding the cost of a 2-use shampoo packet to less than the cost of an egg. Other products they are "educating" the market for: disposable nappies, but only for the night so families can get a good night's sleep or for use during family outings; and feminine hygiene products to reduce stress and provide greater comfort, enabling girls to study better. Not a peep about landfills or biodegradability.

The luxury category

Christian Lacroix was placed under protection from creditors in June. Hadn't made a profit for *22 years.* Downsized staff from 120 to 11, closed down haute couture and prêt a porter, but held onto accessories and fragrance licenses. A luxury licensing boom in progress, especially in specialist or peripheral categories such as kid clothes, swimwear or accessories. Hard luxury products like watches and jewelry had slumping sales. Arnaud said philanthropy is a growing focus of LVMH.

Demand for **Hermès** handbags stayed constant. Does Hermès manipulate the alligator skin market? In the mid 1990s the luxury brand began buying tanneries and in the last few years has become the largest player in the exotic skins business. Bought aggressively from the alligator farmers in

Florida, recently at prices far lower than the past. Rival tanneries accuse Hermès of hoarding, forcing other fashion houses to pay premium prices. Nobody mentioning anything about the environmental damage tanneries cause.

Zegna recrafting their brand, aiming at a new demographic of under 30s. They will stick with menswear, more stable, has more loyal customers. Burberry launched a social networking website to encourage people to share their own trench coat stories. Plaid has its own registered trademark. "Our differentiator," says CEO. People are wearing fragrance less today than previously. A bright spot was fragrance priced at $100 or more, where sales grew. Perfumers now position "noses" as stars of their brands.

Galactic Space Resort says it is on-track to accept guests in first microgravity hotel in 2012. Rack rate: €3 million, for a three-night stay. The single pod will orbit 450km above earth, capacity: 4 guests and 2 astronaut pilots. What, no concierge? Those pilots are going to need training in guest service. Luxury is hard.

Rolls Royce sales grew in 2008. The company is introducing the Ghost, designed to sell higher volume, "less formal than the Phantom and a bit more dynamic," which translates "cheaper", at a price point of €200-250K. Of 8000 select prospects who showed interest, 85% were names new to the brand.

"If a word is worth a coin, silence is worth two." –The Talmud

Unbranding

Last year I commented on Vodafone's rampant brand pollution in India, and the criticism stands. But elsewhere in the world companies like Coca-Cola, luxury names, youth and hospitality brands are exploring *avenues of greater discretion* in their visual presentation. Starbucks took away its logos in their Seattle Capital Hill store, rebranding it like a Mom and Pop coffee place. They'll try anything to preserve their premium image as competitors like McD chip away at market share.

Sayonara

Edward T. Hall, who pioneered the study of nonverbal communication between members of different ethnic groups, died in August. He developed a cultural model that emphasized the importance of *nonverbal signals* and modes of awareness over explicit messages, all interesting ideas for brand professionals to ponder. He looked at cultural attitudes toward space and time as part of the informal realm of communication. *"The Hidden Dimension" (1966)* examined cultural meanings of architecture in a discipline he called proxemics, a kind of proto-place-branding theory. He also explored the use of time as a form of communication, a technique which marketers employ.

Amir Pnueli died in November. He was a computer scientist who applied Arthur Prior's theories of *temporal logic,* propositions qualified in terms of time, into computer modeling techniques. Prior's work explored "tense logic," to evaluate statements whose truthfulness changes over time. Sounds suspiciously like marketing claims, doesn't it?

"On the internet, nobody knows you are a dog." - Anonymous axiom

Adios, traditional media

News organizations remain stymied about how to charge for news online. One publisher comments "we haven't reached an inflection point in attitude." For the time being their position is vague to cautious as they search for ways to cut costs. Various media labs are now testing algorithms that assemble facts into narratives that deliver information, no writers required. Career journalists beware.

Lured by the affordability of e-marketing, seduced by the explosion of social media, and looking to cut costs, smaller firms fled traditional direct mail marketing. US consumers received about 5.2 billion pieces of direct mail in the 3rd quarter of 2009, down from 7.1 billion in the prior year. Some companies saw precipitous drops in business, and had to return to snail mail to recover. Customers said they missed the letters, especially the ones which contained humorous illustrations.

The US market for online advertising is now estimated at $29 billion. AOL abandoning subscription-based service, migrating to advertising-supported digital media company. Time Warner, who divested AOL, are crafting strategies to deal with consumers now using digital sources for news and entertainment. Ad brokers target online display ads aimed at audiences selected for *other characteristics* than age or income. Now they troll personality traits.

Vibe Magazine, which folded under a pile of debt last May planned a relaunch as a print quarterly. New owners InterMedia Partners distributed 300,000 copies, half their prior circulation guarantee. New owner says they can "imagine many ways in which the brand can exist and be *monetized outside its print heritage*." Esquire's December augmented reality cover featured Robert Downey Jr. and a bunch of letters flying off the cover. Not sure anybody noticed. Vanity Fair Italia's print edition is growing in a down market. It's Condé Nast International's biggest magazine in terms of revenue. Uses big photography layouts both original and drawn from archives, and content repurposed from American Vogue, W and GQ. Weekly format, abbreviated mix of news briefs, estimated reading time 6-14 minutes per longest article. Lisbon has a new print newspaper, nicknamed i, short for *infomação*. Looks more like a traditional magazine than a newspaper, and puts the most thought-provoking and analytical writing first. Paid circulation of 16,500 in a population of 10 million. The strategy is to build relevance for the brand in the shortest time, and eventually *expand the name into other media*, the first projected brand extension to be a web site.

Movies outperforming DVDs

Flicks now outpace disks as studios eye a shrinking DVD income stream. They place their hopes on 3-D and mass-market blockbusters. *Avatar* passed $1 billion in ticket sales in the second week of January, with two-thirds of its receipts from abroad. France has an *amour fou* for the new technology, with the most 3-D screens in Europe. *Libération* recently declared James Cameron "galaxy's eco-warrior."

More brilliant ideas from the dinosaurs

Abandonment Tracker Pro alerts a subscribing web store when a visitor puts an item in a shopping cart or begins an application, and then doesn't complete it. Enables an action called "remarketing", where visitor gets a follow-up email or pop-up asking [sic] "Oops, was there a problem?" It may increase sales, or alternately irritate customers who never come back again. No way to measure.

Pepsi announced it won't advertise its drinks in next year's Super Bowl, ending a 23-year run. Launching "Pepsi Refresh Program", aimed at directing $20 million for projects people create to "refresh" communities.

mailorama.fr dreamed up an inspired promotional stunt to promote their brand: a red double-decker bus would drive around Paris throwing cash from the windows. Locations were communicated via promotional buzz on the web. A crowd estimated at 7000 assembled at one location, mostly residents from tough suburbs, poor students, homeless men. Surprise, a riot ensued, police were called in to restore order. Arrests, beatings, damage to property. Company wouldn't answer calls, and later issued a statement saying it was sorry things had gotten out of hand. Donated the €100,000 budgeted for the event to a local charity.

It's no longer who you are

Twitter introducing "geolocation" allowing users to include a precise location with each tweet, thus enabling search limit by location. Users suggested the idea. Little companies are popping up, measuring 'buzz' by surveying *where* trendsetters go. People leave 'data shadows' behind as they move through cities.

Yousef Tuqan Tuqan quotable at the World Brand Congress in Mumbai last November: "What the 50-year old marketing manager knows doesn't matter." "The media is no longer in charge." "Advertising doesn't need the media anymore." "The conversation is going on with or without you."

291,667 people joined Facebook *in a single hour* on January 2, 2010. Last October, 26 million tweets in a day were recorded. Social network participation via mobile devices will increase from 80 million in 2007 to 800 million in 2012. A study by UC San Diego reports US households collectively consumed 3.6 zettabytes of information in 2008. (One billion trillion bytes, or a one followed by 21 zeroes) The huge increase in byte consumption is related to video games. In a single day 100,000 words cross a person's eyes and ears from various channels, web, text messages, video games. *War and Peace* is 460,000 words long. Print media is in consistent decline, but web-surfing means *people are reading more than ever.*

the following touchpoints to debate and discussion for the coming year

"Thank God I'm an athiest." – Luis Buñuel

Increasing co-creation

Hershey and Pitney Bowes set up customer innovation centers to capture understandings of how customers use their products. Companies aren't generally structured to access, absorb or utilize customer insights since they are organized by product, not by customer. Technology companies have been the most active in relying on others to innovate for them. Consumers often come up with ideas, then companies wait at the sidelines to see whether they have mass appeal. Twitter certainly outsources idea-generation to its readers. When people started referring to posts as "tweets" Twitter resisted, until mid-2009 when it finally applied for a trademark on the term. Kraft Australia asked customers to propose a name for its new *Vegemite* product, a salty brown yeast paste mixed with cream cheese, yum. Over 3 million units sold in two weeks to a population of 22 million. The winning name, suggested by a 27-year old designer: *iSnack 2.0*. A wonder Apple didn't say anything. But others did, thousands of Twitter posts, a dozen Facebook groups, and a protest website. Company quickly decided the name was not worth defending, given the level of outrage. Kraft compares this to the failed 1985 New Coke launch, which ultimately served to reinforce consumer loyalty to that brand.

"All great cities are schizophrenic."–Victor Hugo

Where in the world, indeed.

More than 40 million fake Swiss timepieces are made every year, generating profits of around $1 billion. "Made in Switzerland" has so much value that 5000 Swiss brands use their nation of origin in brand marketing, because it implies precision and quality. Now the government plans legislation that demands Swiss share of production costs must be 60% for goods to use the label "Swiss." Country brands are big ships that don't change course quickly. Ina recent article Philippe Mihailovich points out that "Made in China" carries so much baggage that it would be more effective to establish "Made in Shanghai" as a new luxury differentiator.

"Fame sometimes defames good honourable people."
– Portugese Fado lyric

For a change, let's talk about celebrity

US media obsessed for Warhol's designated 15 minutes over the White House gate crashers, a pair of social climbers who then tried to sell their story to the networks and tabloids. A reality TV show Dad perpetrated the balloon boy hoax, which kept the country riveted to their screens watching a home-made UFO drift across the western skies. He then tried to sell his story to the networks and the tabloids, but got arrested instead. In July the world went crazy over Michael Jackson's untimely demise, a false veneration of epic proportions. The Jackson family then sold and re-sold their story to the networks and tabloids. Do we detect pattern recognition here?

Tiger Woods used to make roughly $100 million a year on endorsement deals, his career earnings over $1 billion. After the crack-up Woods generated escalating negative buzz with *women*, who make many of the endorsed product buying decisions. Woods was golf's #1 draw and #1 television ratings driver. Tournaments where he played had 30 million more viewers than those where he did not. The economic impact of Woods' imbroglio on sponsor firms hasn't yet been calculated, though some academics rushed to try. Gillette ran more sensitive statistical tests correlated against share price performance, some of which cleared the *5% significance threshold*. The final insult: Cadillac repossessed the crashed Escalade and plans to do repairs, then sell it as a "used fleet vehicle."

"The better the bad guy is, the better the film is." - Alfred Hitchcock

Ridley Scott in discussions with Angelina Jolie for role in Gucci biopic on Patrizia Reggiani, who plotted the murder of her ex-husband, Maurizio Gucci.

Once upon a time Elvis, Marilyn Monroe, and James Dean were people with brands attached to them. These days they have migrated into *iconic economic entities* which stand for sexuality, voluptuousness and rebellion. Society constantly hungers for heroes. In 2009, heirs of Bruce Lee announced the launch of a production company dedicated to promoting the actor's legacy. Brando trustees have filed 26 separate legal cases since 2003, initiated by a business partnership designed to protect and manage the Brando brand-o. The major conundrum: how to find commerce in the image of a man who was wary of it.

trendseekers alerts

"It's not a lie if you believe it." *-Seinfeld character George Costanza*

Otaku love

A subculture is thriving in Japan, made up of men and women who indulge in real relationships with imaginary characters. It's a subset of the obsessive fandom that has surrounded *anime*, *manga* and video games, attributable in part to the difficulty many young Japanese have in navigating modern romantic life. Fetishistic love for two-dimensional characters has earned its own slang word, *moe*. In an ideal *moe* relationship a man frees himself from the expectations of an ordinary human relationship and expresses his passion for a chosen character, without fear of being judged or rejected. One 37-year old Tokyo man goes on dates with a pillow emblazoned with a two-dimensional picture of a character, Nemu, from an X-rated version of a PC video game called Da

Capo. She is 10, maybe 12 years old, and wears a little blue bikini and gold ribbons in her hair. "When I die I want to be buried with her in my arms."

Uh-oh, the World Car again

Ford announced plans to unveil its new Focus model, a single vehicle designed and engineered for customers in every region of the world, sold under one name, part of a strategic decision to move from a house of brands to single focus on Ford. The gameplan: small, fuel-efficient cars, with technology and safety features to appeal to customers in Europe, Asia and the Americas, premium priced. Ford is betting on the perceived need for smaller, lighter and more environmentally friendly passenger cars. Believes that customer requirements are going to be more the same around the world than they are different. One platform for all markets, tailored to different regions by changing colors and materials. European and American buyers appreciate flair; Chinese consumers, in particular, have more conservative tastes. Its best asset: the Ford brand and its blue oval badge. In the old days, Ford had as many as 20 international ad campaigns. New Focus would have just 4 or 5 ad strategies. "Any variation will be based on the campaign's audience."

Build your personal brand: go barefoot

Discarded flip-flops are one of the greatest environmental hazards on the planet today. Gazillions of them have been manufactured. Toxic to animal reproduction, dioxin contamination in landfills, harmful to people downwind of incineration, cause impairments to the immune system. A significant part of the rising tide of plastic litter stretching down the East African coastline.

Brand resurrection

Polaroid was the Google of its day, darling of the stock market, the place where everyone wanted to work, a stellar growth story, then a spectacular fall, as digital imaging took over. Yet no technology has replaced the tactile thrill of an instant photo rendered in chemicals straight out of the camera. Its name recognition has never diminished- in fact, it's one of the best known brands in the world, up there with Disney, McD and Coke. And a new group of aficionados breathes fresh life into the brand. A Boston-based company owns the name and the patents and plan a relaunch. Inexplicably they have hired Lady Gaga, a pop star, as their new Creative Director. She brings enhanced visibility and youthful cachet, but how adept is she in new-product creation? We'll find out in an instant.

Terminology and concepts entering the mainstream in 2010

Astroturf organisations - fake grassroots organisations originally created by lobbies and special interest groups to disrupt US health care reform hearings.

Augmented reality - superimposing digital information onto the real world, especially in handheld device displays. A massive product design scramble in progress for expanding the retail experience.

Crowdsourcing - using the proverbial wisdom of crowds to accomplish a task. Netflix paid out a $1 million prize for an improved recommendation engine to increase customer satisfaction and generate more movie rental business. See "Prize Economics", below.

Digital archaeology - manipulation of original files from earlier sources, enhanced to be reused in newer iterations. Often applied when digital cartoons are repurposed for 3-D.

Maybe Journalism - computer-generated simulations of what might have happened, like those made in Taiwan speculating about the Tiger Woods car crash.

Ming pai – Pop Chinese term for famous brand-name consumer items

Mirror neurons - neurons in a network that let you feel or respond in a way that is similar to someone else. The biology of empathy.

Net fame - in the recent Japanese film "*Nobody to Watch Over Me*," the term applied to what voracious internet news journalists seek, in collecting information and exposing people's lives to public scrutiny, with no concern for truth or justice.

Prize economics - running a contest to generate a new innovation at less cost than an in-house research and development effort.

The Singularity - the notion of a moment, popularized by the computer scientist Vernor Vinge, when humans will create smarter-than-human machines, causing such rapid change that the "human era will be ended."

Screenager – how marketers regard your adolescent kid.

The Third Cloud - new apps where your smart phone doesn't even bother to communicate with your carrier, it just captures the information you need from other sources nearby.

Virtual physiology - new digital processes which allow you to conceive of how things should be and then let the computer figure out how to do it.

"They were decent. They were strong. And they failed in the most beautiful way you can imagine."
– Italian mountaineer Reinhold Messner, on Dr. Charles S. Houston's doomed 1953 Everest expedition.

What is a brand?

Thanks to those who contributed definitions this year:

"A brand is a name with power." - Pierre LeGouvello
LeGouvello is President of DDB France. Ad agencies still concern themselves with notions of reputation and competition.

"A brand is first a promise, then an experience and ultimately, a feeling." - Aubrey Ghose
Aubrey is CEO of Dubai-based aisBrandLab. Creatives view brands as living in the world of emotions.

"A brand is something you can wake up wanting." – Anindita Ghose

Anindita reports for the Wall Street Journal/MINT in New Delhi. This statement considers the chemistry of desire, what motivates the compulsion to acquire.

"A brand is spot on." - Susanna Dulkinys

Susanna is Berlin partner at EdenSpikermann. Visual identity designers see specificity and simplicity as critical elements of the brand discipline.

"A brand is a relationship." - Yousef T. Tuqan

Yousef is CEO of Dubai-based Flip Media. Digital media practitioners explore the realm of interactivity.

Recently I have thought about brands as *adopted emblems of personal identity*.

2009

"We are healthy only to the extent that our ideas are humane."
–Kurt Vonnegut

"If it isn't broken, break it." –Gossip Girl

We inhabit an era of magical thinking, which could have been authored by Garcia Marquez and Kafka *avec la participation de* George Orwell. An economic collapse in the wake of the election of Obama, followed by the Mumbai incident. It's all too weird. Nobody notices that bottled water costs more than gasoline. Let's learn to relish disorientation. Everyone struggles with how to survive the crisis. But what are we going to do when it's over? How will we know when it's over if we couldn't see when it began? We do a lot of research on how brands succeed, not a lot of analysis on why brands fail. During boom times how many organizations plan for hard times? We need to get better at assessing the true cost, value and consequence of actions, so we're not condemned to live out Santayana's curse. The reality is that fewer brands will exist in the marketplace, it will be more difficult to launch new brands, and we are sure to see more consolidation of existing brands. Get ready for a hyper-competitive environment. In the spirit of the times, the new it-bag is the reusable shopping bag. It's what we will remember as today's slogan t-shirt. Hidden in those not-opulent, not-pretentious bags are the real opportunities for brands of the future.

update on last year's hot topics

Accountability and outcome – For obvious reasons, these keywords push to the forefront of public discussion. Businesses now re-examine their own practices, with the temptation for finger-pointing at the expense of learning any lessons. I'm reminded of the short story by Borges, "*The Garden of the Forking Paths*," which describes a world where all possible outcomes of an event occur simultaneously. As an exercise I often run brand simulations with my clients, playing out multiple scenarios. It's useful to ask: what are the consequences of our actions and how are we prepared to deal with them?

Failure and obsolescence - Accidents are crucial to innovation. They move us past our limits and bring us to outcomes we couldn't produce deliberately. So we need to find ways to build the allowance for accidents into corporate culture. This means acknowledging failure as a necessary and valuable part of the innovation process. We are constrained by the habits, routines and presumptions that constituted earlier behavior. Organisations need to remember that over the centuries researchers have stumbled upon hosts of big ideas while searching for something entirely different. Pfizer Inc was testing Viagra as a heart medicine when scientists noticed an unexpected side effect. Yet one aspect of product-creation hasn't been greatly entertained: the study of obsolescence. This is interesting. The idea of life-cycle in products or brands isn't much considered, not until demand drops. Only then do the post-mortems kick in. A study of conditions that accompany obsolescence is suggested, what abets it, why we create products which ultimately we don't need, the point at which brands outlive their usefulness. I note the recent demise of the Bill Blass brand. Some explanations offered for the label's end: There was an aging clientele, a management that seemed to take a freewheeling approach to the brand and its failure to find a successor who could match the Blass persona.

Of course the end of particular products, brands or hedge funds could simply relate back to the seven deadly sins. Bonus points for those who can cite them by their original Latin names: Lust (*luxuria*); Gluttony (*gula*); Greed (*avaritia*); Sloth (*acedia*); Wrath (*ira*); Envy (*invidia*); Pride (*superbia*).

"Dogs bark at strangers." – Heraclitus, ca. 500BCE

Differentiating branding from marketing and communications - The practice of brand-building is not simply the province of admen and marketers, who represent a fraction of the discipline and tend to distort the understanding of what it is we do. We work at a high strategic level for our clients. Brands are dimensional, living entities which touch every point of stakeholder interaction. Brands will play a bigger and bigger role in business practice, governance, education and theory in the years to come.

"You've got to be honest. If you can fake that, you've got it made."
–George Burns

Doing good to do well - Thomas Gad, Chairman of the Medinge Group, addressed the issue of so-called Green Branding at our annual Sweden retreat in September. He's seen a growing perception of urgent need by his clients for answers in this area. At the same time he reports a fuel of tensions in the marketplace over what it means. Thomas says there's a clash of vernacular, green vs. sustainability vs. organic vs. fair-traded and more. He showed a single slide of different enlightened logos, each representing one of these often-not-parallel agendas. Gad's research indicates that consumers place a lot of hope in technology, and they will more and more seek out what he called climate-marked products. Talk of these high-intention products led me to wonder if an index could be created to validate the claims. Skepticism rules the marketplace, which is why consumers ask for more informative in-store decision-making tools like credible labeling.

It's more difficult to make a virtuous act now that the bottom has dropped out of recycling. Patrick Harris believes our current generation "may be remembered not as the 'consumer generation' as we understand it, but as the 'disposable generation' - one which produced immense waste." Recyclers at present are stockpiling trash- hoping for a turnaround by 2010.

During the Beijing Olympics the momentary impression of a truce, as Coke sponsored the stadium and Pepsi sponsored the recycling, a presumptive cooperation. After the Olympics, the bitter rivals returned to their usual sniping in a newly-declared non-sugar sweeteners war.
Travelers trudging through international departure areas in Heathrow and Hamburg airports the first week of November may have stumbled across booths marked with a big blue Z,

help points set up to offer free Internet access, cell phone and laptop charge-ups, and other concierge-style assistance. It's part of a new marketing campaign from Zurich Financial Services focusing on customers "when it really matters... trying to build consideration and favorability for the brand," said Arun Sinha, head of marketing. Research indicated that fewer than 15% of customers trusted insurance companies. The kiosks do not offer insurance.

New heroes and the cult of celebrity

Paulina Borsook says the only books that reach the nonfiction bestseller list have titles like *Oprah's Chef's Veterinarian's Memoir of Child Abuse.*

NYTimes headline, December 19, 2008: *Mother of Palin Daughter's Boyfriend Arrested*

"It is best to hide folly." – Heraclitus, ibid.

Personal branding

Tom Cruise silent on Scientology concurrent to premiere of new good-Nazi flick, "won't speak about [my] religion publically;" *Roman Abramovich*, Russian oligarch adding the world's largest yacht (168m) to his armada for £200m; *Ali Kordan*, chastened Iranian minister who falsely claimed to hold an honorary degree from Oxford.

Social networking, it's bad! – Video of a Web2.0 presentation by NYU Media prof Clay Shirky circulated around the net. His thoughts on how to deploy the cognitive surplus, the physics of participation, ending with the idea that "People like to consume, but they also like to produce, and they like to share." Believes that social networking in the commercial arena happens *in that order.* Ends with the conclusion "Media that's targeting you but doesn't include you may not be worth watching." Kids already know this, and do any of the actions individually, or in whatever order they like.

Social networking, it's good! – "People are relating to the Americans on the computer. Regardless of political views and what the politicians do, we want to have this kind of cultural relationship with the United States." –24-year old Iranian journalist

Social networking, it's bad! – A demented Mom impersonated "Josh", a supposedly infatuated teenage boy, and drove her daughter's rival to suicide using MySpace. St. Charles County Prosecutor announced there wasn't enough evidence to charge anyone in connection with the kid's death.

Social networking, it's good! – Mizuko Ito, lead researcher on a MacArthur Foundation study swears internet socializing by teens is not a bad thing, "...participation is giving them the technological skills and literacy they need to succeed in the contemporary world... how to get along with others, how to manage a public identity, how to create a home page." 2008

Social networking, it's bad! – At least for advertisers. Facebook ads don't generate the interest or participation expected. The revelation: people who use social networks want to network socially, and not buy into marketing schemes or endorse products.

"Due to the financial climate, I had to make the decision to cancel the 2008 holiday party." – Robert Duffy, partner at Marc Jacobs fashion brand

Devolving luxury – You'll know luxury is rebounding when eyewear begins to move again. It's a sure sign that people have the extra cash for affordable symbols. Timepieces follow, and then those obscenely-priced handbags. May not happen before 2011, though.

"Luxury luggage companies are looking for ways to make their brands stand out from the crowd... Travelers are asking themselves, 'what does this luggage say about me?'" commented Milton Pedraza, CEO of Luxury Institute. Has Mr. Pedraza traveled recently? The experienced traveler does not want to stand out. Luggage simply wants to say, "Don't steal me. Leave me alone." Luxury is now embracing functional products as revenue-generators, stepping back from extravagant items. Prada, Gucci, Fendi, Lanvin and Bottega Veneta have all added luggage brand extensions. Louis Vuitton and Hermès differentiate themselves by offering limited edition or custom-made travel bags.

On 1 December 2008 Hermès ran a color banner ad on NYTimes.com, an act unthinkable two years ago. Luxury has embraced the internet: witness Lagerfeld's recent ersatz silent movie on Chanel.com. Viewing the movie requires a commitment of almost 20 minutes, eons in internet time. When luxury steamroller LVMH cancelled plans to rent a new 10-story building in Tokyo, category-watchers nodded knowingly: 2009 is certain to remain a distressed market.

the following highpoints to debate and discussion envisioned for the coming year

"The greatest source of sorrow is the pursuit of happiness." - Voltaire

BRIC nations

At Medinge's September retreat, Sergei Mitrofanov and Dmitry Petrov opened their panel by making a series of all-inclusive statements about the largest emerging markets in the world, over 3 billion potential-customers-strong:
• That there are already *established brands* in those local markets, of which we of the developed markets are unfamiliar, and that these are the brands with which newcomers will need to initially compete;
• That the BRIC nations have low loyalty to any brands, and are open to new ones;
• That nations in emerging economies are *price-sensitive*, and in search of value;
• That these nations embrace *"luxurious poverty"*, and will opt for single luxury items;
• That those who are *first to market* will have a strategic advantage;
• That *intellectual property* issues will continue to prove problematic until some universal standards of protection are agreed upon.

Quiet brands

Dr. Robert Zajonc, who studied half-hidden patterns that unconsciously inform the ways in which everyone navigates the social world, died on November 30, 2008. He discovered that subjects reliably preferred shapes they had been exposed to the most often, though they had no conscious awareness of the fact. The effect was dear to the hearts of advertisers and other shapers of culture, brand-builders included. Strangely, H.M., the most important patient in the history of brain science, died the next day. Following experimental brain surgery in 1953 to remedy blackouts, seizures and convulsions, he lost his ability to form new memories. As a participant in hundreds of subsequent studies, he helped scientists understand the biology of learning, memory and physical dexterity, and to identify declarative memory, which records names, faces and new experiences and stores them until they are consciously retrieved. He was, I suppose, the most famous brand guinea pig.

"Time and silence are the most luminous things today." –Tom Ford

In Autumn 2008 I traveled widely through rural Rajasthan by car. It made me reconsider the idea that brands need not be so visually prominent to reinforce what they stand for. What about rethinking the idea of brands as healthy instruments of silence? Vodafone has spent an enormous sum plastering its garish red logo on every available surface in India, sometimes at massive scale, in an effort to reinforce its brand recognition by raising its profile. Perhaps the major benefit has been to keep the population of sign-painters and digital banner installers working. In doing so they've despoiled landscapes and unwittingly made a colossal statement that the brand has no understanding of the concept of visual pollution, and low regard for what this incessant barrage does to people, already overloaded with screaming messages. Why does a brand need to be this noisy? A brand isn't just another form of packaging. This is the myth of "eyeballs" or "number of visual impressions" that conventional advertising has perpetuated. Even companies with do-good products offend: Vespas has outsized markings on their wind turbines all over the world: guys, get a grip- nobody wants to see your logo that big. So here's a free, radical, profile-raising idea for Vodafone: announce a new multi-*crore* brand campaign to *remove* all those red logos from every exterior surface in India. Put people to work restoring the landscape, promoting harmony and quiet and beauty, demonstrate that the company, even if its offering is mobile telephony, values the silence in between the use of its products. That would count as a major PR victory, not to mention improve the company's sustainable reputation for years to come.

"We weren't *for* anything. We were against everything."
–John Holmstrom, founder of *Punk* Magazine

Claude Lévi-Strauss turned 100 on November 28, 2008. In light of his work, which took difference as the basis for his study, not the search for commonality, I pondered what brand professionals could learn from this. In Lévi-Strauss' own words, "...societies are progressively integrated into world politics and economy...their relevance has become either documentary or, mostly, aesthetic" and they contain defining contexts "telling not only what they are but what they were meant to be when they were created." The Quai Branly's landscape architect noted that "...[he] represents an extremely subversive vision with his interest in populations that were disdained... He knew that cultural diversity is necessary for cultural creativity, for the future."

"History is a pack of lies about events that never happened told by people who weren't there." – George Santayana

Brands and history - In March 2007,Patagonia fired sponsored ambassador **Dean Potter**, a highlining and BASE-jumping xtreme athlete who has demonstrated an affinity for parachuting from a tightrope or other more stable high places. He had made several controversial climbs, which could be labeled spiritual experiences, if he is not addicted to being watched, since he always seems to have a photographer along. The jury still out on that conclusion. The brand asked him to make public apologies, which it appears he did- debate rages about despoiling climb sites and exhibitionism, two things Patagonia doesn't want to get tarred with. Mr. Potter's latest reported activity is base-jumping from a line stretched across Utah's Hell Roaring Canyon.

Potter's calling isn't anything new. The legendary Jean Francois Gravelet, who performed under the name **Blondin**, repeatedly crossed the Niagara River Gorge on a suspended line in 1859. On one walk he stopped at the halfway point above the falls, and prepared an omelette on a portable stove.

The incredible shrinking page

While the death of analog may be exaggerated, print advertising budgets diminish. In July the prescient Sam Zell, CEO of Tribune Co. lamented that he was "...looking at some of the worst advertising numbers in the history of the world." Tribune declared Chapter 11 in December "...definitely an environment that most have never seen," sighed Ed Ventimiglia, publisher of *Departures*. What's a brand to do? Luxury brands continue –quietly- to spend on client dinners and launch parties, direct client engagement. We'll see more licensing, product placement, unconventional outreach. Amazon's Kindle reader now represents 10% of Amazon's book sales, 250,000 units sold, 200K titles available.

trendseekers alerts

Terminology and concepts entering the mainstream in 2009

Behavioral neurogenetics - A relatively new field "exploring a handful of genes that seem to be related to depression, anxiety, addictive personality, sensation-seeking and other traits. The same article discussed "the booming happiness industry." Beware of the product-creation stampede.

Chimerica - historian Niall Ferguson's term for the de facto partnership between Chinese savers and producers and US spenders and borrowers. Are we talking about "Chi" as in China, or "Chimer" as in chimera?

Citizen journalism - Another iteration of user-generated content in which non-professionals use modern technology and the global distribution of the Internet to create, augment or fact-check media independently, or collaboratively. We saw a lot of this kind of activity on *Twitter* during the Mumbai siege. Especially interesting was how much of the chatter was useless, baseless, conjectural or simply irresponsible. The conclusion:

don't trust anything you read: validate it rigorously through multiple sources.

Cloud computing – Google's dream: a scenario in which people store all their digital libraries and multimedia files online, and can access them from any computer, anywhere.

Coutourisme - a category I have invented for the travel industry, where clients are encouraged to choose destinations purely for the purpose of buying chic clothing.

DMB – (pronounced *"dumb"*?) Digital Media Broadcasting, referring to the explosion of video usage on mobile phones and other mobile devices, an especially hot phenomenon in South Korea, where users watch an average of 15 minutes a day. So far providers haven't found the model to produce big revenues. "Content is time-critical," says a consultant.

Narco-analysis - a controversial technique, banned in most democracies, where the subject is injected with a truth serum. Mumbai police say they're going to use it on their surviving terrorist. Imagine if the focus group guys ever get their hands on this stuff.

The uncanny valley - a challenge identified by digital animators, who have noticed that the more human their characters look, the less lifelike they seem, with eyes often taking on a creepy, zombie-like hue.

White space - vacant TV airwaves being freed up by regulators, clearing the way for next-generation wireless devices and internet services. Fertile territory for products which have yet to be developed, especially in the evidence-based design spectrum, i.e. products for the home, energy regulation, security, inventory control, real-time monitoring.

Wrap rage - The emotional reaction to infuriating plastic "clamshell" packages and cruelly complex twist ties that make products almost impossible to open without power tools. Sends about 6000 Americans each year to hospital ERs with injuries caused by trying to pry, stab and cut open their purchases. Packaging designers take note.

"Every beast is driven to pasture with a blow." – Heraclitus, ibid.

What is a brand?

Seeking a new twist in this section of the letter I'll include some speculative jottings from my own notebook over the past 12 months:

- A brand is an icon of impermanence
- A brand is a marker of time
- A brand is momentum personified
- A brand is by nature obsolete
- A brand is a specific set of attributes connected to a product, organization or place
- A brand is an all-encompassing social construct which defines the vision of an organization or entity.

And the musings of a diverse clutch of interdisciplinary experts:

"A brand tells a story in which the main characters are recognisably the market or audience. With most brands today, the organisation still puts itself or its product at the centre of the story. A powerful brand tells a story that consumers or prospects can easily weave into their own." - Tony Quinlan
Tony is Chief Soryteller for London-based Narrate.com.

"A brand perches on a shelf, and thinks it knows who you are." –Trungpa Bumbleché
Bumbleché is Director of the Self Center, and founder of Luminaries Without Boundaries.

"A brand is an exercise in identifying, organizing and coordinating marketing variables."
- Joao Freire
Joao is a Lisbon-based brand strategist.

"A brand is a searing experience you want to repeat."
–George Rush
George is a New York City-based newspaper columnist.

"A brand is the mark originally left to protect livestock from potential loss and theft. The term now implies labels, logos,

---

artwork and names or words that one can register in order to claim a unique and profitable connection, or forcibly associate with products or services in order to foster favorable feeling."
–Steven Considine
Steven grew up on a cattle ranch near San Diego, California

"A brand is for the masses who don't know better."
–Philippe Mihailovich
Philippe is a Paris-based luxury brand guru and author of the forthcoming "Haute Luxe".

Recently I have thought about brands *as inner journeys in search of tangible points for human connection.*

2008

"The improvement of the world must be highly contextualized."
–Hans Rosling

A strange year musing on brand, with prevailing enthusiasm, increased interest, and an undercurrent of cynicism. Everyone knows they have or need a brand, everyone wants one, yet many people still cannot say precisely what a brand is. One professional I interrogated asked me if I wasn't fed up with it all. "Maybe you should stop querying people about what brands are," he told me. "Maybe you need to find a new term for branding. Maybe you need to give it a rest." I said, "It sounds to me like you are suffering from brand fatigue."

Later, on a visit to friends in San Diego, I observed their 8-year old daughter reading two books about fairies. I asked her to tell me about them. She began by saying, "Well, they are both the same brand," and pointed to the Disney's Fairies logos on the covers. I found it remarkable that a child her age cited that aspect first, using the correct commercial term to qualify her preference. If the child makes the brand differentiation before describing the conceptual quality of the product, could it indicate a case of brand overkill? Brand recognition at the expense of healthy fantasy? Brand valued as more significant than the true, emotional experience?

update on last year's hot topics

Semiotic society - I am still convinced that at their most fundamental, brands are symbols we exchange to discover common territories of understanding among our contemporaries. No conversation is free of them. See how long it takes for a brand –any brand- to surface in a discussion ("Let's meet at Starbucks."), observe how we take ownership of the brand, use it to define ourselves. We adopt the values the brands express, and we use them to contextualize our counterparts. The most successful brands somehow capture essential statements of value. We 'osmose' the brands, then regard them as extensions of our selves. We trade them back and forth to find points of tangency. This set of common beliefs and stereotypes tells our contemporaries who we are, and sheds light on the identity which we recognize in them.

Innovation – Twelve months ago innovation seemed to be taking the lead as a prime area of brand definition. After Apple repeated their winning strategy with the introduction of the iPhone, everyone ran workshops on what could be learned from it. More recently I have heard corporate managers talking about leadership returning to the discussion, the sense that innovation cannot occur without someone at the helm driving the process. Paul Rand told me essentially the same thing 25 years ago when I asked him what he thought was the key to IBM's brand success. He said he couldn't have done any of it without Watson's support. Can Apple score again without Steve Jobs?

Place branding – A prominent American graphic designer says the first thing brand USA needs to fix is "rhetoric". Doesn't mention culture at all. Her favorite media is two-thirds CondeNast-centric: The *NYTimes*, *The New Yorker* and *Vanity Fair*. She also says the eagle is an undesirable national bird: Asks, *"Have you ever been in a room with one?"* Prefers the Statue of Liberty as a symbol. Loves the flag. Israel rolled out a new ad campaign featuring svelte Israeli Army women, Sabra cowboys and tony health spa images; the best place brand news for the country surfaced in January 2008, when Olmert and Peres announced a joint venture with Renault and Nissan to promote electric cars and charging stations nationwide. China has its share of bad news/good news days in the run-up to the Olympics. Pollution issues, the Three Gorges Dam, tainted pharmaceuticals and toxic paint on kid toys. Mickey Mouse in traditional Chinese costume hasn't fixed the problem. The City of London had its own heartache over the UK Olympics logo flap, with Wolff Olins taking it on the chin for their graffiti-influenced signature. Nobody liked it, and its creators defended it. Liverpool showed real progress in its campaign as this year's European

Capital of Culture. Opening ceremony appearance by Ringo brought international attention- the city hopes to attract two million visitors who will boost the local economy by £100m.

Est! Est! Est!

Last year I wrote about the use of words to express incongruity between what might be expected and what actually occurs. Perhaps it is time to name January 7th as International Brand Irony Day. On that auspicious date in 2008 Matsushita introduced the world's 'biggest' flat screen at 150" and Tata introduced the world's 'cheapest' car at $2500, opposite ends of the consumption spectrum. A week later Apple introduced the world's 'thinnest' computer. Companies frequently try to deliver the utmost, stretching our expectations to accept only the extremes.

"I don't believe in marketing. Marketing was a job invented for people who didn't know what else to do." –Karl Lagerfeld

Differentiating branding from marketing and communications - A conference scheduled for February in Barcelona concerns itself with internal branding and employee engagement, and promotes a list of speakers who advocate workforce orientation as the first line of brand defense. Not a new idea at all. What is telling, however, is that most of the speakers come from marketing and communications, which underscores the perpetual dilemma for brand professionals: we are mistaken for marketing types, which is broadly off the mark. At the risk of repeating myself, brand is much more dimensional than simply marketing. Brand concerns itself with a range of issues across the spectrum. If you think that branding is marketing, you are living in the dark ages. On a recent brand audit project some of the following questions were posed: *Is the brand on message? Is the brand in line with the strategy, aims, shareholder wishes, management? Is the brand appropriately structured? Is the brand platform robust & future-proofed? Is the brand present in the organization, in its behavior, at all levels?* So brand needs to be regarded as a strategic tool, a force which informs marketing and communications.

New heroes and the cult of celebrity

A.O. Scott, writing in *The New York Times* on November 21, 2007, commented, "From Andy Warhol to Lonelygirl15, modern media culture thrives on the traffic in counterfeit selves. In this world the greatest artist will also be, almost axiomatically, the biggest fraud." This brings to mind the tragic example of the truly unremarkable brand named Britney Spears, relentlessly goaded by insatiable sensationalists. She, her mother and unfortunate sister deserve to be left alone- not debated, hounded, discussed, idolized or reviled. When the inevitable crash occurs, the media will discover itself complicit in her destruction. There's little humanity left in her battered brand, now that a web site is taking bets on the date of her death. Poor Britney long ago ceased to be a real person. She has been reduced to inanimate status, simply an economic entity there to enhance the incomes of her handlers, managers, record companies, and the tabloids.

Personal branding – A recent research survey reported that 40% of Americans now have tattoos, indicating that a "tipping point" has been reached. More proof: a national chain of tattoo parlors is slated to open in 2008.

"The children now love luxury. They have bad manners, contempt for authority; they show disrespect for elders and love chatter in place of exercise." – Plato, 392 B.C.

Social networking –The behavior evolves. In days past, if you did not have a presence on the internet you did not exist. Next, web cred was contingent on a MySpace page. Today your existence is defined by a Facebook page, which has trumped YouTube as the digital watering hole. A new add-on at Facebook enables pageholders to build vast, networked games of Poker, Life, Monopoly, other group amusements. Friends compete virtually. I just read an article in the local Seal Beach paper, whose young author encourages people to game on Wii as a weight-loss strategy. How one regulates one's social networks also evolves. An 18-year old female asks a 20-year old male friend for his IM name. He gets evasive. Later he says they can message through Facebook, a less intimate, more public interaction.

"The possibility of loss is what makes things valuable."
–Wallace Stevens

Luxury

The ever-adaptive luxury category experienced another year of transformation, growth and record profits. With rumblings of recession, the low end falters, the fallout after luxury's attempt to garner downmarket clientele. The weak Yen has dampened the Japanese market. But the top tier responding to 10%+ growth continues to offer even more expensive products, which account for 25% of luxury sales, fueling the hyperluxury category. Hermes reports third quarter '07 profits up 12%, attributable to exotic leather goods performing well in Europe. Luxury also learned to love the web, after initial resistance to the medium. There's a degree of unevenness to brands' sites (Has anybody looked at the Hermes site lately? It can't be helping their surging numbers.) In a white paper authored for *CondeNet*, Dee Salomon cites several brands successfully exploiting web-based videos: Chanel messaging through style.com mobile phone feature, Cartier using its video assets to pull users to its LOVE campaign on its website, Marc Jacobs allowing fans to populate a virtual field by planting a signature daisy which grows when its owner interacts with the site. And all eyes are fixed on Tom Ford, to see if there really exists the business to propel his ambitious launch into high-end, branded bespoke couture.

the following highpoints to debate and discussion envisioned for the coming year

Accountability and outcome – These are the new critical buzzwords when talking over sustainability and CSR. In a January 7 special section, *The Economist* again discounted the practice of corporate social responsibility, arguing that profit was a company's first objective. (Did anyone read Gates' speech at Davos urging companies to get more humanistic in their conduct?) The section also cited the famous December 2006 *Harvard Business Review* paper by Michael Porter and Mark Kramer on how, if approached in a strategic way, CSR could become part of a company's competitive advantage, deconstructing the practice into Strategic CSR and Reactive CSR. What with improved transparency, greenwash is a lesser probability. Constructive change is seen as the result of "disruptive innovations," a term I like very much. In a paper I recently authored with Thomas Gad, Scandinavian companies are examined for their sustainability practices, in place for two decades or more. In Scandinavia, CSR is expected as component part of organizational policy. Companies now return to emphasizing their core values and product attributes in brand-building.

Anatomy of a trend – Ever wonder why advertising now appears on the packing materials holding your new technology purchase? In 2007 clever marketers saw YouTube videos of people "unboxing" their new Xbox game consoles. (There weren't enough units to meet the demand- lucky folks shot footage of how they unpacked their new toy and posted it online.) Immediately our friends in the Marketing Department seized on the opportunity for a new venue. Reminiscent of those POP video monitors at the airport, bank and grocery store, which do nothing more than add unwanted visual and noise pollution to a crowded environment.

Measurement – Didn't take long: researchers are trolling the social networks, surveying, sampling, building their graphs and pie charts. Next they'll be interrupting your mobile phone calls.

"I find I have no faith, none at all, in progress. I do not expect a better future... I pray that I am wrong, but nearly every amenity of life has declined in my lifetime. Only technology has improved, and even technology disappoints, breaks down, and is impossible to get repaired." – Arthur M. Schlesinger, Jr.

terminology and concepts entering the mainstream in 2008

Gériatruc- A Franglais term I made up to describe products created especially for the aging population. This reflects the trend towards a renewed interest in design. Expect products with larger typography, better legibility, ergonomic design, easy to hold and operate, rounded edges. In apparel, accessible pockets, bigger buttons, easy closures.

LEE7-Speak – Pronounced "*leet-speek*", homonym-based internet argot, which fuses numerals and letters.

Telepresence - According to *Ask Dr. Nerd*, this is what's so great about the new killer app "Halo", which replicates or somehow synthesizes eye contact during video calls.

Transcreation – A concept reported in the October 16, 2007 *Wall Street Journal*, which describes the retrofitting of Powerpuff Girls cartoon characters specifically for Japan "…designed with one audience in mind to [really] resonate in another culture." Essentially, fiddling with the brand to cultivate another territory.

WiMax – a next-generation wireless technology which enables Internet and other data connections across much broader areas than Wi-Fi. Allows a device to hold a connection while in motion via signal handoff from antenna to antenna.

What is a brand?

Or better yet, what is attractive about them? After all, brands have a certain allure, a particular bravado which appeals to us. They express personal affinity, consequently brands are tools of self-expression. This contradicts the idea of a brand as something *externally* driven. In fact, the idea of brand has morphed into "something inside me."

This year I queried a wider group of practitioners, whose replies, as always, lend tantalizing controversy to the ongoing debate.

"A brand is a kind of engine that creates energy." – Pierre d'Huy
Pierre is a principal in eXperts consultancy of Paris, and a Director of the Medinge Group.

"A Brand is the Truth, revealed over time in numerous ways."
–Mike Keeler
Mike Keeler is a former ad professional who edits the often-acerbic
Quicksilver newsletter.

"A brand is sometimes cerebral and sometimes emotional, [an idea] which sometimes makes a simple statement of key attributes and sometimes triggers a complex burst of emotion by association." –Manas Fuloria
New Delhi-based Fuloria is a recognized authority on supply chain economics.

"A brand is a wooden idol." –Joshua Berger
Josh is a founder of the Plazm design studio in Portland, Oregon.

"A brand is the DNA that separates a product from a commodity."
– David Michaelson
Dr. Michaelson is a principal in a New York City-based brand research firm.

"A brand is unwilling to commit to its future... or at least a future that is propitious."
–Michael Marckx
Michael is VP Brand and Strategy for Globe International, a footwear manufacturer.

"A brand is what allows people to have a conversation around a product even when the product offers nothing remarkable."
– Filippo Dellosso
Dellosso is a strategic planner for Chiat Day, based in Paris, France.

"A brand is a mindset." –Sascha Löetscher
Sascha is a principal in the Zurich office of graphic designers Gottschalk+Ash.

Recently I have thought about brands as memes which express common beliefs.

2007

"Whatever the Party hold to be truth *is* truth. It is impossible to see truth except by looking through the eyes of the Party." - George Orwell, *1984*

update on last year's hot topics

CSR morphs into - Even a feeble attempt at a hatchet job by *The Economist* couldn't kill it. Brands now understand they need to demonstrate corporate social responsibility, and all the big players have bought into the idea. Still, many organisations ignore it as a part of their brand strategy. Perhaps the phrase itself sounds outdated, stuffy, do-gooding, not-too-compelling. Today we are more concerned with *sustainability*, and that is the present replacement term. But the meaning intended by the introduction of sustainability was 'systemic'. In other words, *practice systemic intervention*. The death of advertising – rumors greatly exaggerated, as long as we agree that advertising represents a fraction of the discipline of branding.

Luxury – Luxury brands squeezed at both ends? Counterfeiting soars, due to record low-tier demand. On December 14, 2006, the *WSJ* reported that in the past 2 years the port of Antwerp, Belgium alone has seized 40 million counterfeit items, a fraction of the estimated $500 billion in illicit goods traded globally every year. The high end now seeks *"extreme" luxury*. That means things like very expensive custom tailoring will soon be available in Gucci boutiques, with the appropriate costs for one-offs and superior customization. "This is the new buzzword this season to describe objects at a tipping point of price, production and quality that places them well above the mere expensive gifts. It is aimed at a new aspirational category of clients," said Suzy Menkes, in the December 8, 2006 IHT. At this writing, the luxury travel category is developing extreme products like space tourism which will occupy the high end of their market for the next ten years. The luxury segment was conservative about entering the web, but lured by clever marketers the category now buys *bundled packages* integrating traditional print, broadcast, and new media along with the internet, just like Target. Another fertile terrain: luxury *brand extensions*. Bulgari has demonstrated exceptional flair in this area, adding its brand so far to fragrance, a resort, a luxury automobile and a commissioned novel. That's style.

Measurement –To quantify a brand's value, people tend to go first to Interbrand's yearly list, so I append the link to it here: www.ourfishbowl.com. It is worth a read to see how big business contextualizes itself, kind of the Oscars of international brands. Their methodology is based on "revenue" and "influence" and "demand" factored against conventional metrics.

What about considering a brand's value based on some of the following web-based and humanistic criteria:

- Number of links to or from its home page
- Number of links on its site to other appropriate resources
- Number of times its name appears in or links to the relevant blogosphere
- Linguistic mapping
- Evidence of the brand in social networks
- Depth of user-generated content

Just asking.

the following highpoints to debate and discussion predicted for the coming year

Differentiating branding from marketing and communications – Before I gave a speech last year I received a letter, a portion of which said: "We need to make sure [you] understand [branding] is not about broadening membership, but about broadening our consumer's desire and ownership. I think they specifically want a full court press for US market penetration." *Brand isn't just marketing.* A brand is more deeply dimensional than an instrument used solely for market penetration. A brand builds relationships, many of them beyond the point of purchase. A brand is a link to shareholders, employees, vendors, competitors, friends, neighbors, legislators, journalists, industry analysts, folks who don't use your product or people downstream who won't want your product or service for another 5 years. *Marketing is a small part of branding.*

new terminology and concepts entering the mainstream in 2007

User-generated content – YouTube and MySpace pioneered the phenomenon, which is best realized by youth brands. Even Charles Saatchi has a site for student art, with *3 million hits a day* and over 20,000 artists participating. This season Conde Nast launches a new teen-oriented site originated by its own community of reader/contributors.

Flogs – Watch out for these *fake blogs*, which look like the work of real bloggers or smart viral marketing, but aren't. They're just the schemes of sneaky people trying to appear authentic as they sell product you probably don't want.

Web 2.0 - The next 'dot com' boom?. Firms specializing in these unique technologies (a large number driven by online gaming) rich with venture capital are moving back into the ghost town that once was San Francisco's Silicon Gulch. The keyword here, according to AskDrNerd, is *"Collaborative"*. Don't get burned

Sustainable tourism – the only place tourism has left to go. Eco tourism can sometimes be too rough for the time-challenged but cash-rich upscale traveler, so the category is creating products which reinforce their lofty values in higher denomination top-end branded experiences. These combine culture, comfort and sustainable concepts, a quiet revolution in the industry. Thought leaders try to stay low-profile as they deliver personalized, unpackaged travel with a conscience, mindful of the impact of development on communities, the necessity to preserve legacy and heritage, while leaving a minimal footprint. Most importantly, it affords eco-tourists an opportunity for guilt-free total immersion in the real culture of a less-traveled place.

New heroes and the cult of celebrity

I'm a big admirer of Sicco van Gelder's *Global Brand Strategy*. In it he identifies Reputation Brands, those driven by the notion of heritage or myth. It's especially significant to consider personality-driven brands in the world (and particularly the USA) today. Consumer society has become overly focused on this type of brand. We think we "know" the person, so we accept the endorsement or adopt the cause, often without the due diligence. Entertainers and sports figures accustomed to high-visibility often become seduced by their own images, and we encourage them by our obsession with their divorces, children, lawsuits or political advocacy. It's time for some new heroes, people like Dean Kamen (developing a low-cost, portable water purification system), or Branson (devoting £400 million to renewable fuels over the next four years), or Anousheh Ansari (who visited the International Space Station and came back to encourage cross-border sharing of new technologies), or Aung San Suu Kyi (under perpetual house arrest for championing human rights in Myanmar). These 'reputation brands' can be judged by their actions, and not the output of their press agents, or the amount of bandwidth they occupy in international media.

Semiotic society – Today we inhabit a society driven by symbols. We exchange symbols to define who we are to ourselves and each other. People no longer buy products, they buy symbols, represented by the brands we adopt. Symbols express values and meanings. Symbols perpetuate beliefs and stereotypes. Symbols are the DNA which govern brands. In the marvelous idiom of French intellectual deconstruction, cultural legend Régis Debray coined the term *Mediology*, which analyzes the "higher social functions" (religion, ideology, art, politics) in their relationship with the means and mediums/environments [*milieux*] of transmission and transport. Worth a visit: **http://www.regisdebray.com/**, to delve into his musings on how cultural symbols migrate.

Place branding

If you disbelieve that a nation can be branded, consider the case of Kazakhstan and a mockumentary created by the

British comedian Sascha Baron Cohen. Simon Anholt, quoted in the November 24, 2006 *Newsweek*, "Surviving Borat," said that he could not believe Cohen wasn't on the nation's payroll for his role in bringing so much attention to that little-known country. Anholt rates countries' brand value by looking at consumer indices- see http://www.nationbrandindex.com/about.phtml. The movie itself is a weird hybrid, kind of a combination of "Jackass" meets the "Jerky Boys", making much with stereotyping, and the humor of victimization. My opinion of Cohen elevated when he claimed he was unable to contact Borat, who -he reported- was "attending the Holocaust Denial Conference in Teheran." Nation branding has definitely been brought to the forefront by this odd cultural quirk. According to Malcolm Allan, at placebrands.net, a nation brand can 1) enhance or damage a place reputation and identity; 2) characterize how places operate; 3) attract or repel talent, inward investment and tourism; or 4) promote places in their markets. These seem to be the prime drivers (both negative and positive) in place brand creation. So let us now celebrate Kazakh oil, carpets and cashmere. And wish them a boost to tourism.

Personal branding

or how to contextualize yourself, in brief:

The Events Leading Up To My Death -title to the unfinished autobiography of Preston Sturges
That Wonderful Book on Plague -working title for a colleague's autobiography
The Memoirs of an Amnesiac -title to the autobiography of Oscar Levant

The end of irony?

"Borat" got me reflecting about how irony was so absent in the new media world, how utterly literal and mindless criticism has become. In the interest of invigorating the discussion of brand statements, here are some definitions of classic, Socratic intellectual forms which have fallen out of understanding, authoritative use, or perhaps fashion:

Irony - The use of words to express incongruity between what might be expected and what actually occurs.
Satire – wit used to point out social ills, or to effect change
Sarcasm – ostensible wit, often purely hostile, used to convey disdain or scorn
Parody – mindless wit used simply to poke fun
Allegory – symbolic lessons cast in narrative form

Creatives move east – And not exclusively to Asia. Romania needs a CBO for a large media company, global salary. An LA-based ex-identity firm (now respositioning itself as brand consultant) wants a pitchman they call a Brand VP, largely a sales position for Asia, with a base salary of $125K plus incentives. There are more jobs to be had than people to have them in Asia today. A great deal of talent has already migrated there. Previously a product would have been marked "Made in China." Soon the label will read "Created in China."

Innovation – You hear this word a lot more, from all categories. Recently a major turnaround at the French brand Carrefour was attributed to "innovation." The CEO of Marks & Spencer credits their resurgence to the same thing. Two years ago theory held that brand rested on a tripod of strategy, leadership and creativity. But the equation has changed, and many practitioners today add innovation, naming it the attribute that keeps a brand competitive. In order to innovate, there must be a corporate culture which allows room for it.

Branded conflict

An interesting year for politics, in light of a new branding phenomenon observed. The most visible branded conflict was an incursion into a country on a path to reconstruction after decades of civil war. Depending on whose account you believe, Hezbollah's abduction of Israeli soldiers provided the justification/provocation for the wanton destruction of much of the Southern Lebanese infrastructure. Long before the Israeli army marched in, Hezbollah had branded their cause "The Divine Victory", with a Swiss-graphic-inspired logo, attached to a well- thought-out, absolutely artificial, mindful, calculated brand program. It was a conflict which Israel could not win with military muscle. As soon as the bombardment ceased, propaganda signage on the rubble instantly appeared with the logo applied, and the same signature plastered on yellow plastic police tape strung across the ruins photographed for world media. When Najibullah resurfaced he was filmed on a background of the same logo, and the same week the *IHT* dutifully reported in a headline that "Hezbollah claims Divine Victory." Here is a political movement successfully deploying the tools of branding. The world views these details and thinks them innocent. The poorest nations now know how to manipulate their images. Such complete calculation shows this could not occur by accident or chance. We are not prepared to meet well-thought out constructions like these, the antithesis of humanistic branding.

What is a brand?

It is often the first question I am asked. Last year at the end of my letter I listed some concepts that have been put forth over time by my colleagues in answer to this inquiry. This year a group of new voices offers their own definitions. I also append a brief profile of each speaker.

"A brand is a 'once upon a time'." –Pierre d'Huy
Pierre is a respected Paris-based brand consultant, and a Director of The Medinge Group.

"A brand is the most powerful business tool." – Thomas Gad
Thomas is Chairman of The Medinge Group, and recognized international branding authority.

"A brand is social capital." – Ava Hakim
Ava works in large-scale global business development for IBM.

"A brand is a shorthand for all the reasons people choose the products and services they want in their lives." – Simon Paterson
Simon is a world-class London-based brand professional.

"A brand is the good name of a product or organisation." – Malcolm Allan
Malcolm is an expert in place branding, leadership and strategy.

"A brand is the emotional response or preference for a product or service." – Tom Atchison
Tom is a venture capitalist with an interest in the commercialisation of space.

"A brand is what you elect to live and breathe."
– Patrick Harris
Patrick is a London-based brand and strategy guru, and a Director of The Medinge Group.

Recently I have thought about brand as an understanding which delivers a personal sense of identity or purpose. Or perhaps an *opportunity for systemic intervention?*

2006

Interviewer: What do we need to make things right?
Buckminster Fuller: Integrity.
Interviewer: That's all?
Buckminster Fuller: Necessary and sufficient.

update on last year's hot topics
Corporate Social Responsibility – Still at the forefront of dialogue, and essential to successful branding. A proven, winning strategy, despite some skeptical press. The fact is, larger companies all have included CSR in their business plans. If it's absent, something looks awry.
Sustainability - The ecology of conduct. A key to clear brand-building.
Retention – Companies get this by consistent delivery of promises.
Valuation – Last year I postulated that the internet and events were the best venues for applying conventional metrics about brand's value. Recently there has been talk about correlating brand value and internet performance. See this article from IHT, January 2, 2006:
http://www.iht.com/articles/2006/01/01/business/ad02.php

the following highpoints to debate and discussion predicted for the coming year

On contemporary brands -
John Cage reported a story about a visit with Isamu Noguchi: 'There was nothing in the room (no furniture, no paintings). The floor was covered, wall to wall, with cocoa matting. The windows had no curtains, no drapes. Isamu Noguchi said, "An old shoe would look beautiful in this room."'

I believe there is room in the commercial space for ugly brands. I believe that brands are a journey, living entities, organic, fractal, and grow at their own rates no matter what grids or matrices or order or values we impose on them. I think the iPod is fraudulent packaging of a small chip, with high principles of functionality added in. People were prepared to pay a premium for the feel good aspect of the product. I think the aesthetic of Mad Max is more authentic, while the aesthetic of iPod is seductive veneer.

The war will be fought between veneer and content. Any aggressive, intrusive carrier prevents the content and meaning of a brand to get through. We have the choice to look at brands idealistically or cynically.

Our task is to reinstate a harmonious chorus of ideals.

I believe that the most meaningful brand interventions occur person-to-person, and that advertising as we knew it in the past erected a psychological barrier between the stakeholder and product, service or institution. The most powerful brand statements are made human-to-human. Thoughts on the death of advertising

Neoadvertising will nurture interpersonal branding.

One of the great pollutants of the modern world is noise. Advertising is an inorganic population of the natural environment. A healthy dose of silence would be good for the collective consciousness. In the future, advertising will maintain a lower profile and speak in a softer voice.

Did anyone see the article last June in the Wall Street Journal about Universal's promotion of its remake of 'King Kong'? A 2 ½-minute teaser ran simultaneously at 8:59:30pm on June 27, on 9 networks owned by their parent company: NBC, USA, SciFi, Bravo, CNBC, Telemundo. This is what is popularly known in the ad business as a "roadblock." What would be the strategy to create a "thoroughfare"? In this scenario the advertising doesn't accost you and stop you in the road and hit you over the head. On a thoroughfare stakeholders understand, discriminate, opt in or out, and go on their way unimpeded. Old advertising is just thin icing. The most effective new avenues are
- personalized
- free of psychological artifice
- interactive
- authentic and sensitive
- unobtrusive
- diverse
- and quieter

I wonder if the greatest disturbances to the natural/organic environment are the most extreme examples of advertising today. What the future demands is quieter, individualized statements, which afford us elegant choices.

Luxury rebounds – the luxury category has definitely rebounded, by necessity a category compelled to continually reinvent itself. We buy luxury goods primarily to assert our own identity and individuality, attaching the brand's attributes to ourselves. "This is me." The category is exhibiting a lot of co-branding (jewelers owning hotels, couture making housewares for chain stores, fashion brands accessorizing high end automobiles), and much in partnership with tourism, a growth category. May be some correlation to the graying of the population and the demographic's access to disposable income- more time shares, vacation homes, property-related ventures.

Primary advocacy - The most resonant brand statements are made by primary advocacy, face to face, person to person. So a primary intent of branding may be to promote people telling other people directly one-on-one about a brand's promise.

Guerilla Marketing – Historically this referred to employing unconventional approaches to market, targeting key influencers and early adopters. But people are more sensitized or used to this technique – especially in some categories (technology, music, apparel and footwear). Thus, it's now become old news, predictable, not unusual, and best employed judiciously.

On-demand media and products – continue the trend in customization and personalization, what Eric Pfanner called the "*youniverse.*" It is also smart economics, utilizing just-in-time delivery strategies. Previously this was largely the domain of luxury brands- but technology now enables mid-range brands to offer greater flexibility of product delivered. Brands transit the digital world, acting as talismans of meaning in the landscape. People have become prisoners of the internet and mobile telephony, even though it's just filters. We constantly check our personal communicators, using them to massage interactions and validate ourselves. All this to oppose the isolation technology often brings.

What is a brand?

Everyone knows they need one, but people still can't say what it is. I'll close this letter by listing some concepts that have been put forth over time:

"A brand is a promise." –Ian Ryder
"A brand is a conversation." – Stephen Rappaport
 "A brand is the symbolic glue [that holds people together.]" – Colin Morley
"A brand is the means through which an organization symbolizes, differentiates and communicates itself to all its audiences." – Jack Yan

Recently I have thought about brand as a locus of intention and action.

2005

update on last year's three hot topics

Corporate Social Responsibility – Most of the big players have jumped in and devoted resources to demonstrating their social relevance and connection to community. The best examples can be found in smaller institutions –like Patagonia and the John Lewis Partnership- who built their brand around CSR as integral to their process. A cover article in the March 19, 2005 *Economist* sought to debunk CSR by arguing it was good for some business models and less important for others. My opinion is that organizations still ignore CSR at their own peril. The market is fickle, shrewd, well-connected and quick to switch loyalty.

Transparency – A brand's viability is often judged by what surrounds its statements of transparency. Consumers proceed from the assumption they are being lied to, especially with numbers. All the fancy balance sheets in the world may not obscure mindless conduct by an organization disconnected with an understanding of the breadth of its stakeholders. One bad experience can travel better than ten good ones

Sustainability still reigns high in the pantheon of brand values. Consumers are demanding that people of all kinds gain productively from a loyal relationship over time.

the following highpoints to debate and discussion predicted for the coming year

Authenticity looks to continue as a prime brand driver. Brands seek credibility outside the jargon. Action here speaks louder than words, but action entails risk.

"Risk buys spontaneity. Only in spontaneity can you be authentic."
- Tai-Chi Master

Diversity - The youngest brands in the world are making this statement in their core values, and it is a powerful indicator of a generation's collective consciousness. For brands to succeed in the world of the future they must translate across cultures and allow for differences in habit.

Brand is fertile terrain for renaissance people. Brand is interdisciplinary. Brand is the networking of the cosmos. Brand is about the conscious efforts by groups of people to fashion shared understandings.

Recognition and Differentiation - I believe that at least one way brand manifests itself is at the moment of recognition, when some abiding impression is formed or reinforced. If the job is done well, one brand can authentically be distinguished from another. Then the choice is in the hands of the consumer.

Retention was noted last year as an aspect some businesses were concerned with improving. The consumer products sector needs to develop long-term loyalty. NGOs need to sustain participation and awareness. What would we get if the NGOs started to develop consumer products? Just asking.

Think Global/Act Local - Still proving to be a brilliant, relevant and effective maxim. It is utterly important to understand local sensibilities and culture. The era of imperialistic brands is over. The next generation of stakeholders consider themselves part of a world community, but they like their own home towns.

Valuation - People still need to know what the tradeoff is for the money spent. One could begin with conventional metrics like survey; sales figures tracked to a particular product; eyeballs. I still believe the paradigm of value for branding lives outside the usual raw B-school numbers, which are available. It's difficult to define the value of 100 million well-disposed brand ambassadors. How much is a fully motivated, branded-within workforce worth in dollars these days? In pesos?

The event industry seems to offer more opportunities for brand metrics than other channels, since there is so much possibility for personal engagement and captive observation. This may suggest that people-to-people communication is the richest type of brand impression, and that removing the insulation of media from between stakeholder and organization allows for quality interaction, not to mention better metrics.

Online branding promises expanding brand measurement opportunities, in fact the internet may be the first mass medium built for automated measure and modeling of predictive behavior. With this comes the usual potential for fraud. Take, for example, "clean hits," the gold standard of online marketing. We've seen the birth of sinister enterprises manufacturing, reporting and charging for bogus hits. A similar phenomenon has occurred in "keyword auctions", where vendors bid for hierarchal placement, choosing keywords based on their popularity. Here manipulators artificially inflate the market by bidding against themselves to drive up auction prices.

2004

The first brand letter sent. In August of 2004 I emailed a very basic memo to my client list, addressing a set of questions received from them over the course of 2002-2004. These are the answers given:

Is it better to maintain one global brand or many different local brands?

Brand Architecture
How an organization structures and names brands within its portfolio.

There are three main types of brand architecture systems: *monolithic*, where the corporate name is used on all products and services offered by the company; *endorsed*, where all sub-brands are linked to the corporate brand by means of either a verbal or visual endorsement; and *freestanding*, where the corporate brand operates mainly as a holding company, and each product or service is individually branded for its target market.

In favor of the single brand, tremendous economies of scale.

Against the single brand, difficulty in creating personal connection with the consumer.

B2B products seem more susceptible to global branding Regional brand equity often trumps consistency, particularly if the product serves a very traditionally-minded market segment.
How far a brand can scale depends largely on how much the brand touches *a particular culture's values*

Consistent branding around the world seemed a desirable but not essential goal
Of course a global brand would be ideal
The reality is, you cannot write off the equity in your market
While global brand consistency may create more value for the company, it also generates greater risks. For example, it threatens effectiveness of local market recognition.

All public relations challenges are potentially global. A problem anywhere can very quickly turn into problems everywhere. It is important to *react immediately.*

Quality control is a key source of risk for the global company. Silence is seldom golden, especially in the information world. "For firms that are second or third in a market, taking risks is a way to get ahead."
Peter Singer, Brookings Institution, July 2004

Sustainability- people of all kinds gain productively from a loyal relationship over time

Volatility- most people lose, and a small number profit by opportunistic behaviors

UN-accepted definition of Sustainable Development: development that meets the needs of people today without compromising the ability of future generations to meet their needs.

Valuation of Marketing from Chris Macrae

1. Biggest customers and exit customers – the strengths of your context's segmentation
2. Most profitable customers and newest strategy implementation customers
3. Average customers and customers it would be most valuable to learn with
4. Most needy customers and most complaining customers – highest risk + responsibility group

Thanks to my faithful readers, contributors, collaborators and co-conspirators

Stephen Barber, Filippo Dellosso, Dr. Manas Fuloria,
Tim Goodwin, Fritz Gottschalk, Pierre d'Huy,
Christopher Lindsay, Sascha Lötscher, Michael Marckx,
Simon Paterson, George Rush, Pascal Somarriba,
Yousef Tuqan, James Wines, Michael Wolff, Jack Yan

and to Dolce Paula - perfectly branded.

www.ingramcontent.com/pod-product-compliance
Lightning Source LLC
Chambersburg PA
CBHW060831170526
45158CB00001B/134